POSITIVELY HAPPY

NOEL EDMONDS

POSITIVELY HAPPY

Vermilion
LONDON

Visit Noel's website: www.noeledmonds.com

Noel Edmonds Worldwide Representation
John Miles Organisation Email: john@johnmiles.org.uk

5 7 9 10 8 6

First published in the United Kingdom in 2006 by Vermilion,
an imprint of Ebury Publishing
Random House UK Ltd.
Random House
20 Vauxhall Bridge Road
London SW1V 2SA

This edition published in 2007 by Vermilion, an imprint of Ebury Publishing.

Random House Australia (Pty) Limited
20 Alfred Street, Milsons Point, Sydney, New South Wales 2061, Australia

Random House New Zealand Limited
18 Poland Road, Glenfield, Auckland 10, New Zealand

Random House (Pty) Limited
Isle of Houghton, Corner of Boundary Road & Carse O'Gowrie,
Houghton 2198, South Africa

Random House Publishers India Private Limited
301 World Trade Tower, Hotel Intercontinental Grand Complex,
Barakhamba Lane, New Delhi 110 001, India

Random House UK Limited Reg. No. 954009
www.randomhouse.co.uk

Papers used by Vermilion are natural, recyclable products
made from wood grown in sustainable forests.

A CIP catalogue record is available for this book from the British Library.

ISBN: 9780091917227

Cover designed by Two Associates
Interior by seagulls.net

Printed and bound in Great Britain by Cox & Wyman Ltd, Reading, Berkshire

Copies are available at special rates for bulk orders.
Contact the sales development team on 020 7840 8487
or visit www.booksforpromotions.co.uk for more information.

To Charlotte, Lorna, Olivia, Alice
and in memory of Dudley and Lydia Edmonds

CONTENTS

ACKNOWLEDGEMENTS

To Maria Robertson - heartfelt thanks and enduring gratitude for your support, commitment and love beyond the call of duty. I would like to thank my agent and friend of over 30 years, John Miles, who was so influential in persuading me to return to television with *Deal or No Deal*, and my personal assistant Gaynor Love for taking on yet another project and for turning my rambling thoughts into legible notes. I am extremely grateful to the editorial team at Vermilion, especially Clare Hulton and Imogen Fortes, for this opportunity and also for their invaluable advice and guidance throughout the process.

In acknowledging my gratitude to those who have provided so much encouragement, support and love in recent years I am fearful of unintentional and serious omissions. So this acknowledgement is certainly not exclusive and I apologise to anyone who feels ignored and unappreciated. Hopefully you understand that in a book about positivity this is most certainly not my intention. In particular I wish to espress my heartfelt gratitude to: Mick D, Phillip T, Tom B, Paul N and Terry C, Ulrik and Judy, Mike and Rosie, Andy and Catherine and Mike and Frankie.

Finally I wish to acknowledge that this book is the result of a true partnership with an exceptionally talented writer, Lena Semaan. Her dedication, energy and humour have been remarkable. Lena has broadened my own appreciation of the power of positive thought.

PROLOGUE

I AM, BY NATURE and nurture, a positive person. Of course I have had lows, particularly in my personal life, where failed relationships have caused me considerable anguish and the loss of loved ones an enduring sadness. My resolve has been tested on many such occasions throughout my life – but my positive attitude has always seen me through.

However, it wasn't until I read a description of 'cosmic ordering' in Barbel Mohr's book, *The Cosmic Ordering Service*, that I realised my outlook on life was a positive one. The book rang some bells with me in terms of its fundamental belief that you have to ask for what you want, rather than sit back passively and wait for it to come. Mohr's book concentrates a great deal on something she calls 'cosmic ordering' (that you can ask the cosmos for what you want and it will deliver). I also believe that you will live a happier, more contented existence if you take a positive approach. That means not just waiting for life to happen *to* you but actively defining your goals and creating opportunities so that things will start to work *for* you.

The difference between positive and negative people is that the former are able to take a positive approach *even when life is not going well.* This is essential to positive living. After all, it's easy to be positive when everything is going your way. But our real tests, and the moments that define us all, are those times when we are really up against it. People who can take a positive approach in the darkest and most difficult moments are more likely to bring increased happiness into their lives. They are less likely to be tossed overboard by life's crises because they've made a conscious effort to take the view that there is always something to be salvaged, no matter what.

Which brings us neatly to the fundamental question: what is the cosmos? Does it conflict with prayer? Do you have to sit cross-legged, with beads round your neck, eating only lentils to believe in it? Will your children think you've gone mad?

I believe that to be positive in this life you need to believe in something that supports your own practical actions and efforts. I've always had a very strong faith but have become increasingly disillusioned by conventional religion. I am happy to go to church with my family to celebrate the key events of the religious calendar and I think that many of the ways I behave towards others adhere to what some call 'Christian principles'.

By 'cosmos', I don't mean the universe, because we already know that exists. I'm also not imagining something along the lines of Jason and the Argonauts, where hairy gods in flowing robes beam out from behind soft, puffy clouds and direct our destiny. The literal meaning of the word is 'well-ordered whole' and 'ordered system of ideas', and that sums up my understanding of it. It's not something I can see or touch and I can't prove to you that it actually exists, but then neither can we prove that many of the things we believe in actually exist. All I know is that my belief in the cosmos helps to give my life some sort of order. It's the spiritual backup for all my practical actions and efforts; a positive force that helps me and provides me with a reference point when those practical challenges get damn difficult. The cosmos may be there for me, but it won't deliver unless I set myself goals, make opportunities and believe in my own abilities. And if I do all those things, I believe the cosmos will reward me. Not every time. Not immediately. But I believe if I try to take a consistently positive attitude to life it will pay off.

Without a positive attitude I would not have been able to achieve the tremendous highs in my professional life that I have attained. No matter what the challenge, I always believed that I could succeed. Fundamental to that is the core belief that I have a right to be happy, to fulfil my obligations to myself, to be successful, to love and to be loved. I believe that you 'reap what you sow', and that if you treat others well, they will do the same for you.

Radiate positivity – even when things are not going well – and you will attract opportunities. This, in turn, translates into mental, physical and spiritual well-being. In my darkest hours, my attitude, inspired and encouraged on many occasions by those closest to me, has carried me through to a place from which it has been possible for me to regroup emotionally and adopt a fresh mental approach.

Now, I'll be the first to admit that my upbringing helped me to be positive. If you have two loving parents focused on giving you constant love, security and opportunity then, truthfully, what more could you want? But the fact is that as we get older even the most solid starts in life can be negated by environmental factors. Equally, people who've suffered intolerable hardship can overcome it to become successful, productive and happy.

I want to make it clear that this book isn't about achieving constant happiness every day of your life. That is unrealistic. You are bound to have unhappy and difficult moments, but the way you emerge from these will be determined by the way in which you approach them. Positively happy people accept these moments as a natural part of life. They don't allow their lives to be dictated by negative occurrences; instead they accept them and, if possible, take control. Otherwise they don't waste energy fighting their lows – because they know these moments will eventually pass.

The point is this: even though life can be tough,

unforgiving, frustrating and sad, you can still take a positive approach when dealing with it. And there lies the key to 'positively happy' living. It's the belief that you have a right to love, security and opportunities but also an understanding that you will be challenged in your bid for those precious things. Your mission, should you accept it, is to turn yourself into a person capable of living positively, no matter what.

I've written this book partly in response to the hundreds of people who've contacted me since I've returned to television. Many of them have asked why I decided to come back to the small screen, how I've managed my life in the past six years and what it is that makes me so positive. I guess this is understandable when you consider that for many years I figured prominently in the TV schedules and then, suddenly, I was gone. Sure, leaving television affected me, but it wasn't the worst thing that has happened in my life. My beloved father's agonising, protracted death from cancer was a particularly dark period. I honestly struggled to find anything positive about this great man's final battle for life. To be present when my parents said their good-byes to each other after 48 years together was a deeply painful experience. However, I drew strength from their love for each other and their vow to 'meet again', and I pledged to be an even greater support for my mother and to strive to be a good father to my own children.

Do you want to be positively happy? First of all, you really have to want to make a commitment to actively changing your life. If you don't then, I'm sorry, this book is not going to help you. If you want success and love and the happiness that goes with them, you can't wait for others to bring them to you. Being truly, positively happy only comes from proactively pursuing what you want to do. You are the one with the vision and only you have the power to bring it to life.

I would also add that you should not expect to find in this book the kind of self-absorbed introspection that many other books of this type often propose. First, I'm not qualified to send you to that place. Second, I think that too much navel-gazing creates more problems for people than it solves. While self-focus is at the heart of improving your life, that in no way includes selfishness. Self-focus is about giving yourself the space to fulfil your personal goals, just as you encourage your loved ones to do the same. I also believe that our interactions with others are essential to happiness. To approach the world with the attitude that it's all about *you* may make you successful in material terms but it's not going to make you happy.

And while we're on the subject, bear in mind that I am talking about *your* idea of happiness. There is no point pursuing some universal notion of happiness because it just doesn't exist. Your happiness is a product of what matters to you. If money matters to you then, fine, money may make you happy. However, if it does not and you pursue it at the expense of, say, freedom, or fulfilling your emotional needs, then you will end up unhappy.

The intention of this book is to show, in some small way, how my positive relationship with the world around me has greatly improved many aspects of my life and helped me through others. It might work for you, too. Whether it's dealing with hardship, improving your personal happiness, eliminating your fears or gaining personal and financial success, you can do it.

I hope that this book will empower you to take control of your own life and be **Positively Happy**!

Noel Edmonds

CHAPTER 1

CREATE OPPORTUNITIES AND LUCK WILL FOLLOW

LET'S TALK ABOUT this idea of 'luck'. I think too much emphasis is placed on the belief that luck is a random concept. That is, the notion that one day you will be 'chosen' and your life will change miraculously. Random luck can be a fluke, a raffle, the right bingo numbers or a win at the races by a first-time punter. Sure, there's a tiny percentage of people who seem to lead an incredibly charmed life. But most people who succeed in achieving their chosen goals do so because they create opportunities – not because they have 'good luck'. And because they've taken a positive approach to life, life often rewards them with some extra good fortune. This has nothing to do with random luck; rather I believe it's the cosmos recognising a person's determination to strive for opportunity.

The vast majority of people who experience success in one of its many forms do not sit around waiting for life to happen to them. They're not the types who believe all their problems would be solved if only they could win the lottery, inherit money or marry well. They are the ones who actively set out to make things happen. And they don't do it just because they have to; they do it because they want to achieve something meaningful. Sometimes they will know exactly what they want. At other times they will pursue a more indirect route by trying out different things. Successful people also tend to be risk takers. By that I don't mean doing anything death-defying but rather taking a chance on something that feels right to them, without knowing necessarily where it will lead.

When I began taking helicopter lessons I had absolutely no prospect whatsoever of owning my own helicopter. I just had this overriding desire to learn to fly a helicopter. In the late 1970s, even a second-hand Jet Ranger helicopter cost a cool £¼ million and hourly running expenses were in the region of £200. This was big money by anyone's standards! Yet I was determined to fulfil the vision I had of myself flying solo into a London heliport at the controls of my own aircraft. (The details were quite precise – right down to the company logo on the side of the helicopter by way of sponsorship.)

Following my qualification as a pilot, it took over two years for the vision to turn into reality, but it really did happen. Through my interest in powerboat racing, I met a wealthy entrepreneur, Ray McEnhill, who also loved helicopters but who had no ambition to become a pilot.

CAT sitting

We worked out an arrangement whereby he purchased the helicopter and I covered the operating costs. So he got the benefit of having his own personal rotary transportation and I fulfilled my dream of flying myself around the country to engagements. The sponsorship money that I generated more than paid for the operating costs so everybody was happy (except me – I was deliriously, stupidly happy!). It was an unusual business arrangement that came about because I took a chance on something I believed in and created that all-important opportunity. If you set out your intentions and show the cosmos that you are willing to make an effort and take a risk, you too may find your faith repaid in many ways.

DON'T GIVE YOURSELF LABELS

We all know people who seem to be lucky no matter what their situation. They find a good parking space where there had appeared to be absolutely none. They land their dream job. They finish a relationship and then, not too much later, they meet someone else. In fact, just like in the movies, they always get their girl (or guy) in the end. So they get the cream while you're left staring at a carton of milk that's past its use-by date, muttering things like:

- ★ **That never works for me.**
- ★ **I never win anything.**
- ★ **I'm just unlucky.**

- ★ **There's no point.**
- ★ **I never get what I want.**
- ★ **I can't do that.**
- ★ **I've always been that way.**

Meanwhile, your self-professed 'bad luck' hasn't gone unnoticed. Your family knows about it. Your friends know about it. In fact, they've heard about it so often that they no longer call you by your given name alone. Instead, when they talk about you, they say things like, 'Have you seen poor Anne lately?' or 'Bob seems to have an awful lot of bad luck.' When you meet, they greet you with phrases like, 'How are you Bob, you poor thing?' When you're not around, instead of thinking about all the fun they've had with you in the past, they somehow end up saying, 'I feel really sorry for Bob. You know, nothing ever seems to go his way.' And everyone shakes their head and has another drink and thinks how awful it would be to go through life with such (apparent) 'bad luck'.

The advantage of behaving like this is that, secretly, you really like it because – let's face it – nobody is expecting anything of you. By not creating any expectations, you can just sit looking down into the hole you've dug for yourself. The difference between this attitude and that of positively happy people is that the latter never passively wait for the job or the relationship to walk in through the front door. They behave in ways that make things happen. If things don't go their way they try to put a positive slant on events. They don't simply resort to saying, 'I'm unlucky'.

While you might take a job rejection as a major setback in life, they would think, 'Well it probably wasn't right for me anyway. I'm sure I'll find a better one.' For them, setbacks are perfectly normal events. In fact, some people actually use such problems as a launch pad to rocket them to something even better. Being able to change your responses so that you react positively to events is not only healthier but also generates more energy, which ultimately gives you much more chance of creating opportunities. And the more opportunities you create, the more space you leave for good luck to knock on your door. But she's not going to turn up if you don't send out the invitations.

If you want the cosmos to smile upon you, the first thing you need to do is stop thinking of yourself as the 'unlucky one'. I want you to set aside all the limitations and labels you have put on yourself. Instead, clear your head of everything you have thought about yourself. Now you are going to become Bob or Anne 'Mark II' – the new, improved version, ready to take on new challenges and create opportunities. This means you will stop expecting things to go wrong and making self-defeating statements. You have to tell yourself that you have the right to a loving relationship, own a home, change your career for the better, do anything you want to do. You have the same chances as millions of others. The question is, what are you going to do about it?

When you walk through a storm... invite good luck to come with you

I am not a Liverpool supporter but, like many other football fans, I watched the Champion's League Final of 2005 and sat transfixed as Liverpool came back from an impossible position to level the score and then win on penalties. If ever there was an example of cosmic intervention, this was it.

On paper, it shouldn't have happened. I'm sure that even the most die-hard Liverpool fans would agree that Milan was the better team. And 3–0 up at half-time, the Milan players certainly looked dominant. But something magical must have happened in the Liverpool dressing room at half-time. We do know that the Liverpool manager, Rafael Benitez, made some team changes. We saw those. They were clever but, honestly, you couldn't really expect Liverpool to fight back against an opposition of such class. We also know that the Liverpool fans kept singing (unlike some football supporters whose team is in that position, the Scousers did not go silent). We can be pretty sure that someone in the dressing room would have said something along the lines of, 'Pull one back, if only for the fans who've paid so much money to be here'. But I honestly don't think the Liverpool players really expected to win from that position. They just had to carry on playing their best for the sake of their own self-respect.

Going into the second half, nobody could have predicted what was about to happen over the following 20 minutes. The Liverpool players should have come onto the pitch as if they had the world on their shoulders. But they didn't. And then everything changed. The captain, Steven Gerrard, scored a goal. Having created one opportunity, Liverpool found another and added a second goal. Maybe the match could be saved after all. Liverpool then scored a third. AC Milan was stunned. The Italian players would need to dig deep if they were to save themselves the embarrassment of squandering a three-goal lead. The match went to extra time and Liverpool was on what could only be called 'a lucky streak'. The goalkeeper, Jerzy Dudek, became a hero as he was forced into making one brilliant save after another. As luck smiled on Liverpool, the Milan players began to look increasingly tired and just couldn't seem to finish off the opposing side when they had the chance. Liverpool's win on penalties capped what must be one of the most extraordinary comebacks ever. It showed that, even when things look to be against you, if you set out to make just one opportunity, luck can indeed follow.

FOLLOW YOUR PASSION

I feel very lucky because early on in my life I knew that what I wanted more than anything was to be on radio. While studying for my GCEs, I would listen to the broadcasts from the pirate radio ships moored all along the Essex coast. I fell in love with the whole concept of radio. It seemed such an exciting and powerful way to communicate. In much the same way that some people are motivated to write, all I wanted to do was address a microphone. As I studied, day-dreaming of exam success, I also spent a lot of time figuring out how I was going to get near that microphone.

I had absolutely no idea where to begin. Coming from a family to whom the entertainment industry was completely alien (both my parents were teachers), I knew no one in the business who could give me some insights. I did know, however, that the USA had a huge radio industry, so I took myself off to the US Embassy in London to research the subject. Needless to say, I was overwhelmed by the magnitude of the task. Eventually I tracked down a few names and sent letters to a dozen radio stations. They all responded but, unsurprisingly, none of them was interested in an inexperienced English youth.

The BBC would not even grant me an interview. The Corporation didn't need to trawl for potential talent – after all, this was the late sixties and the BBC could have its pick of broadcasters with proven experience from around the globe. So there was little opportunity for a spotty oik from Essex. Meanwhile, I kept bombarding the pirate radio stations with tapes that I made in the tiny studio I'd created for myself in a small corner of the bedroom. None of the pirate stations ever responded directly but one day, while listening to the pirate station Radio London, I heard Ed Stewart make a reference to me. Later that week, on the same station, I heard my hero Kenny Everett tell two of my jokes. At least I knew my tape had arrived!

In the summer of 1967, The Marine Offences Act was passed, which closed down the pirate radio ships (with the exception of Radio Caroline, which carried on for some years longer) and it seemed that my dream of entering the world of broadcasting was now doomed.

I had done just well enough in my A levels to be offered a place at university reading philosophy, psychology and sociology (there was no 'media studies' course in those days!) and was all set to go. I had accepted that that was what I would be doing for the next few years but I still hadn't given up on the radio dream entirely. And just weeks away from starting at university, I received a phone call that was to change my life. It was from Tony Windsor, or TW, as he was known in the days of pirate radio. He had been the senior disc jockey on Radio London and – incredibly – he had retained my amateurish tape and – even more incredibly – he still had my telephone number. He was now tasked with hiring two new disc jockeys for Radio Luxembourg (a land-based European station) and he had to complete the job for a station re-launch at the end of September. I was offered an audition and, thankfully, I passed. Unlike the other candidates, I had zero radio experience (apart from the hours spent making my own tapes in that little bedroom in Romford, Essex) but I had all the self-belief and enthusiasm in the world.

The pirate revolution

Although the sixties was a time of major revolution in pop music, there were few outlets for the latest hits. The BBC was quite old-fashioned at the time and had yet to launch Radio One. For young listeners, eager to hear the latest sounds, Radio Luxembourg was the sole outlet. It was only available in the evenings and had poor reception, but it did play popular hit music. Many pop managers were frustrated at not being able to get their artists airplay. Ronan O'Rahilly, who represented the singer Georgie Fame, heard about offshore pirate radio stations that had been set up around the coast of Scandanavia and decided to establish his own station. He purchased a vessel called the *Frederica*, which he fitted with studios, a 165-foot radio mast and two 10 kW transmitters at his family's port in Greenore, Southern Ireland. He renamed the ship the *MV Caroline*, after US President John F. Kennedy's daughter. In the Easter of 1964, O'Rahilly dropped anchor three miles off the coast of Felixstowe and commenced broadcasts as Radio Caroline 199.

Radio Caroline employed many of the DJs who were later to become household names, including Roger (Twiggy) Day, Simon Dee, Johnnie Walker, Keith Skues, Dave Lee Travis, Tony Blackburn and Tommy Vance. Radio Caroline was so popular that within months of going on air the station had more listeners than BBC radio. Soon, other pirate stations began broadcasting, including Radio London, which launched the careers of Dave Cash, Ed Stewart and Kenny Everett, among others. Pirate radio stations were located just outside UK territorial waters – the two-mile limit, as it was then – and therefore in international waters and so beyond British law. They were untouchable until a new law was brought in to close them down. With the exception of Radio Luxembourg, the pirates remained the only commercial stations broadcasting to the UK until later radio licensing reforms allowed new stations such as Capital Radio to become established.

I loved being on Radio Luxembourg and launched myself into it with gusto. But unfortunately I approached my job with a little too much enthusiasm. Unlike today's DJs, we were not supposed to personalise our slot too much! I'd had two warnings about my (then) anarchic talk between records. Luxembourg didn't want any chatter since the record companies were paying for the airplay and they wanted nothing to taint their artists. I decided to leave Radio Luxembourg before I was pushed. In those days being fired was rather a serious event and my father didn't like the idea of that happening to me.

When I left Radio Luxembourg, in the spring of 1969, I had no job to go to. I returned to live with my mum and dad and, in some respects, I felt like I was almost back to square one. But I was still pretty upbeat and soon an agent who I'd met a few months previously told me he knew someone at the BBC who could help. That person's name was James Fisher and he was a senior executive at Radios One and Two. He seemed impressed with my attitude. At last I was able to show the mighty BBC that I could do something useful for them, albeit for a few months only. I think my determination to work for them really helped. I also think (and certain people may find it difficult to believe this) it was my humility that made the difference. I was just so damn desperate to work for the world's greatest broadcasting organisation. In fact, I was so keen that I accepted a job at £7 a week (contrast this with the £4,000 per annum that I was paid at Radio Luxembourg. This was an absolute fortune when you consider that my dad, the head teacher of a large school in Essex, was getting barely half that amount).

DON'T STOP BELIEVING

In many respects, this was one of the most challenging periods of my life. I'd got my first break and, like most young people, I wasn't really sure what was next. When the pirate radio ships were closed down, it meant there was a huge number of radio DJs desperately looking for work – many of them with far greater experience than I had. But, thanks to James Fisher and his belief that I was capable of achieving good things, I was given a job in his department making programme trailers and competitions for Radio One. This gave me the opportunity to be around the studios at every hour of the day, perfectly legitimately, and I quickly set about making myself as useful as I could. I was absolutely positive that one day this approach would produce an opportunity and, sure enough, it came when Kenny Everett contracted flu. (So often in my life incredible coincidences like this have occurred.) With just 24 hours notice, I had the opportunity to present his Saturday morning show and I was over the moon! I was terrified but utterly delighted! Despite the fact that I'd worked for this moment, I had to keep asking myself if it was real. I knew I wasn't in Kenny's league (I don't think many people were, the man was a genius) but I figured that as the BBC executives had given me this opportunity they must at least have thought I could make a decent go of it.

A few months later, Kenny caused BBC management to see red when he made what he would probably have regarded as a throwaway comment after a news broadcast. They sacked him and I was offered the chance to take over his time slot. I won't deny that this was a stroke of luck. I was in the right place at the right time when the BBC decided to fire Kenny. But if I'd never set my sights on a radio career or done everything I could think of to show people how willing I was, I would never have been at the BBC originally when Kenny got the flu. And yes, because things were going well, maybe luck decided it was worth coming to the party as well.

While I never really stopped believing in myself, I can tell you that there were several moments of self-doubt. Just like anybody else, I'd wonder if I was good enough – even when people told me that I had done well. The important thing was that I didn't let that doubt take over and become reality. I just got on with the job. I think that putting your head down and getting on with it is often the best antidote to uncertainty. If you think about things too much, the gremlins will creep in and destroy your self-confidence.

Deal or No Deal and the wildebeest effect

I see the power of self-belief all the time when we're recording *Deal or No Deal* (*DoND*). I also see it crumble. For people who aren't fans of the show, *DoND* probably looks like nothing more than a piece of light entertainment. But without wanting to over-intellectualise, I think that, for many of our contestants, *DoND* can be a life-changing experience – whether they win big or not.

DoND is a show that thrives on tension, much of it provided by the banker. For some people, the existence of this unseen presence is enough to send them spiralling into uncertainty. Others rise to the challenge. One thing that all of us who work on the show have noticed is something that I call 'the wildebeest effect'. What happens is that somebody will play a bad game. This will be followed by another bad game. And another. It's as if something has seeped into the air and caused our contestants to abandon their own instincts and follow the herd. You can see someone's behaviour change from confident to extremely unsure.

This is then followed by a cycle of contestants who are extremely decisive and positive. It's true! It's as if they've reacted against what happened before and believe it is their turn. Just as in life, if you really do believe, then good things will eventually come. Yes, I know it's all random and if it's not your lucky day you're not going to win the quarter of a million pounds. However, it is noticeable – and indeed it is a matter of game play record – that those who arrive with a positive attitude do better than the nervous, the cocky or the greedy. The relationship with the banker is at the very heart of the game. While I've never heard him use the term 'positivity', if the banker believes that a player has come with a positive attitude, he is more likely to make meaningful offers to that person. And isn't this what life is all about?

MAKE PEOPLE WANT TO HELP YOU

I believe that a large measure of luck came my way because I worked hard to create opportunities. I had an aptitude for what I wanted and it obviously helped that I wasn't setting myself a totally unrealistic goal by trying to be, for example, a singer. At the same time, however, there was no doubt that there were plenty of other talented people around who could easily have got in ahead of me. It's just the same if you go for any job interview. You know that everyone else will have similar qualifications and, let's be honest, any one of them could do the job equally well. But on the day, one of the candidates (hopefully you) proves that he or she has that something extra, that desire and enthusiasm – just the right amount – that the interviewer is looking for. And despite the fact that all the candidates look great on paper, only one will stand out.

Some people might call this chance and, to some extent, it is. However, one thing I have noticed throughout the course of my career is that people will help you only if they feel it's worth it. The more people see you as someone who attracts opportunities, the more attractive you will seem and the more they will want to help you to succeed. Call it a virtuous circle if you like, but it works. If people feel that you are worthy of their help, they will go out of their way to open doors for you. So the more you are able to convince the people with influence that you are indeed worthy of some of their valuable time – and that you can help them achieve what they want – the more likely it is you will get what *you* want out of life. I don't believe I could have sustained such a long and varied TV career if the producers and directors with whom I worked hadn't really wanted to see me succeed. Believe me, it is incredibly easy to attract the support of others if you yourself are positive and radiate success. After all, who ever wants to be associated with failure?

This brings us back to the point I made earlier about not calling yourself 'unlucky'. People who are successful and influential – the people who can give you a job or help you bring a business idea to life – are not going to be impressed by someone who believes they're unlucky. For example, a bank manager is more likely to hand over a loan or agree a mortgage if you look like you're on top of your game. If you walk in saying how desperately you need something, then he or she is likely to take 10 points off your score immediately. But if you go in full of excitement and possibility (even if, deep down, you are not feeling like that) there is no question but they will view you in a more favourable light.

Having identified what you want – a new career, someone to back your business idea, an affordable home, a publisher for your novel – it's time to think about everyone you know who can help you to achieve your goal. Bear in mind the following:

★ **Making opportunities and creating that elusive piece of luck means you need to use the power of numbers. You need to find out who others know who can help you get closer to your goal.**
★ **When you do meet the ones who can help you, be as positive as you can and say that you'd like to ask them for their opinion on what you should do. Remember, everyone is flattered if you appear to value their opinion.**
★ **Even if it's not what you want to hear, show interest in what they're saying. Remember, though, it's a two-way street. People who can help you will want to be sure that you'll do the right thing by them, too. If they think you're going to let them down they won't even bother with you.**

I've always had a very strong work ethic. It cannot be an accident that by working hard – harder than most around me – being reliable and professional day in, day out, the same people offered me even greater professional challenges.

The world isn't picking on you

What if you're really not on top of your game? Ah... Well then you'll just have to pretend that you are. You have to put on your best clothes, smile and remember that others are in the same position. Do you really think that everyone else feels fantastic all the time? Of course not! You're not the only person to be nervous about, say, making a speech, or walking into a big event wondering what everyone will think of you. Attend a job interview and I can bet you that all of the other candidates will be feeling as nervous as you are. One of them probably could hardly get out of the shower, another might even have thrown up.

I have taken part in the Royal Variety Performance and seen major stars rush to the toilets because they were sick with nerves. These were highly accomplished performers who were used to appearing in front of very large audiences – yet the big occasion still got to them. The difference between stars like these and others who fold under pressure is that their experience has taught them how to act confident and in control. That's what you have to do if you're up against it – act the part. Just tell yourself that you have to go into that difficult meeting and give the performance of your life. Take comfort from the fact that when you are safely home, you will be able to let it all out. As they say in showbiz, the trick is never to let them see you sweat.

SHOUTING WON'T GET YOU HEARD BUT MANNERS WILL

Projecting a positive air comes naturally to some but the knack can also be acquired. Here I want to draw a very clear distinction between behaving with confidence and being a cocky show-off. Over the years, I've worked with many individuals who feel the need to dominate every aspect of the proceedings from the car park to the make-up room to the after-show drinks in the hospitality room – or Green Room, as it is known. You don't have to have the loudest voice or the most dominant personality in order to make it in the world of broadcasting. In fact, because TV and radio are a team effort, that kind of personality can actively work against you, especially if you alienate the production team, upon whom you are totally dependent. Respecting people and showing humility is essential – no matter where you are.

This extends to not making judgements about who 'matters'. The fact is that everyone matters. If you're a young person trying to find your way in the world then the best piece of advice anyone can give you is never, ever assume that the most important people are the ones who get paid the most money and have the most impressive titles. Don't make value judgements about who you should be pleasant to. The cleaner deserves the same respect as the chairman. I can't emphasise this enough. You might be the cleverest and most accomplished person in your field but if you alienate people none of that is going to matter. You could become known as, say, 'that person who is rude to the receptionist'. Pretty soon word will get around and you could find yourself on the wrong side of the people with the big offices and the expensive cars who you had been at pains to impress. Good manners will endear you to people in a way that all the qualifications in the world will not. Throw in humility, charm and enthusiasm and you're halfway there. The old cliché 'be nice to people on the way up because you'll meet them on the way down' is so true. I can name at least a dozen of today's senior executives whom I first knew as runners, production assistants, pluggers and researchers.

It is a fact that you never know who in the team is actually going to go on to really great things. We used to have a lovely researcher on one of my shows. Her name was Helen Fielding. I believe she went on to write a book or two and now lives in Hollywood!

MAKE THE MOST OF YOUR MOMENT

In those days radio was a fantastic breeding ground for TV and many people got their start that way. My big TV break came when I was invited to become one of the four regular presenters on *Top of the Pops* (*TOTP*). This was another extraordinary twist of fate because I replaced Ed Stewart, the DJ who had been instrumental in my big break in radio. My first appearance was far from a great success – in fact, a number of friends said I looked about as attractive and interesting as a waxwork dummy that had been left out in the sun! After my initial not-too-promising appearance on *TOTP* I improved very quickly and people noticed that I might have something to offer the visual medium.

It was a time of huge opportunity. There followed a string of shows for the BBC that were very personal and important to me, beginning with the chance to present the *Multi-Coloured Swap Shop*. This came about in a most remarkable way. I had been asked by the BBC Children's Department to present a six-part series called *Z-Shed*, which was all about children's problems (by today's standards, pretty tame stuff). During one live show, a studio light failed spectacularly and, in the middle of a link, I was plunged into darkness. It seemed logical to me to walk to the other end of the studio that still had light. I continued presenting the show as fluently as I possibly could.

Apparently, this minor drama had been noted by senior management, who at the time were casting around for a presenter for a revolutionary new Saturday morning kids' show. My ability to deal with a live problem had not only impressed someone but secured for me one of the most important jobs in television. *Swap Shop* went on to define 30 years of Saturday morning children's television and put me on the map as a television presenter. (I'll be forever grateful to that faulty studio light.)

My biggest stroke of luck!

When I recorded my first show for Radio Luxembourg I had what can only be described as my biggest stroke of luck. The station intended to call me by a name that they already had in a jingle package – 'Randy West'! This was common practice in those days and was the reason that Mr John Ravenscroft ended up being called 'John Peel'. Johnny Walker acquired his radio name in a similar fashion and there were a number of other examples. Thankfully, the station boss, who would have had the final decision on whether I went on air as Randy West or Noel Edmonds, overstayed his liquid lunch. We had to make the recording and so the engineer and I took the decision to stick with my real name. How different things might have been. Would the BBC have hired a presenter for the *Multi-Coloured Swap Shop* who each Saturday would say to millions of children, 'Hello! I'm Randy'?

Making the most of *your* moment means being prepared, even when you're going through a difficult period and your best laid plans appear to have stalled. You don't know when that all-important phone call or invitation to a life-changing meeting will come. So the best thing you can do is be ready. That way, you will never be able to say, 'I had my big moment – but I wasn't prepared.'

The world is not divided into lucky or unlucky people. Just those who think they are. If you want to be among the lucky ones you need to:

- ★ **Take responsibility for your own happiness.**
- ★ **Stop labelling yourself as 'unlucky'.**
- ★ **Believe in your ability to create opportunities and be prepared to take action.**
- ★ **Develop a positive exterior, no matter what you're feeling inside.**
- ★ **Show respect to everybody you meet.**
- ★ **Be prepared to make the most of the life-changing moments when they do happen.**

CHAPTER 2

TAKE OWNERSHIP OF YOUR LIFE

IF YOU WANT to feel truly in control of your life, then you have to take responsibility for it. That means understanding that you have an obligation to yourself to live the best life you possibly can. You can't do that unless you focus on your needs and make space for them. Let me be clear about this. Being self-focused is not about being selfish. It does not mean thinking you are the most important person in the world. It's simply a matter of recognising your right to think about yourself and your needs. It's saying, 'Hang on, I am a special person. I am allowed to be happy in what I do. I am allowed to consider my own happiness as well as that of the people around me. And I am allowed to do all of that without feeling guilty.' You're probably thinking, 'Me? Am I allowed to have all that?' Of course you are, but first you have to claim it.

Do you always need other people to believe in you before you act? Do you always feel the need to seek the approval of others for your actions? While it's fine to ask other people's opinion occasionally, it's not a good idea to be totally reliant on them. The more you're influenced by what others think of you, the more you will become dependent on them for your sense of self-worth. That's fine if they will always be around to tell you what you want to hear. But what if one day they're not there to prop you up? And anyway, what if they don't tell you what you are expecting? Are you going to abandon your dream?

There could be many reasons why family and friends may be negative about your views. Perhaps they are worried about you or have their own dreams for you. They might even feel threatened. The woman who tells friends that she's going to lose weight will often find that they respond by saying things like, 'But you're lovely as you are.' Is that what they really think, or are they simply afraid that that person will succeed where they did not? Another reason for taking ownership of your dream is that you can't expect everyone else to be as enthused about your goals as you are. That's just not the way human beings work.

One of the hardest things to do is set aside the expectations that others have of you. How do you get past the idea that it's wrong to put yourself first in order to pursue your chosen path? I discovered just how hard this was when, at the age of 17, I had to wrestle with one of the most gut-wrenching decisions of my life. It was a decision that, while it would certainly increase my own possibilities for happiness, would potentially mean disappointing someone else and perhaps even making that person unhappy. That someone was my father, a man whom I loved and worshipped. He was someone who, along with my mother, had made enormous sacrifices in his life so that I could go on to higher education and who was overjoyed that I had managed to win a place at university. Meanwhile, all I wanted to do was work in radio. Now, here I was, holding an offer from Radio Luxembourg and wondering how the hell I was going to tell my parents that university was off the agenda.

If that was the only issue, I might not have been sitting in my room feeling sick to my stomach. But there was something else that was really playing on my mind. In the 1930s, my father had badly wanted to go to university but couldn't afford to. His father (who was a very accomplished engineer) had suffered financial troubles and there were no grants available in those days. On top of that, my parents had been so supportive and kind. How could I do this to them? So I'm holding the key to my dream career in my hand and thinking of how awful I'm being in letting my parents down. But I knew what I wanted. Somehow I managed to get the words out. And you know what? My father just said, 'Go and be happy.' He put aside his own aspirations for me in the most unselfish way and gave me his blessing. I don't think any parent can do more than that. To this day I still think about how he must have been weeping inside, but he never let me see it. Now, with my own children wanting to make their way in the world, I understand how hard it is to be a parent.

Maybe your partner and/or children are not immediately supportive when you announce that you're going to, say, take a business course at evening classes. Maybe your best friend will be a bit put out when you say, 'No, I'm afraid I can't come around for our usual chat today, I'm off to the gym.' Perhaps your work mates will give you funny looks when you announce that you're not going for a drink with them after work because you want to spend time with your family. Whether they intend to or not, your friends, family and colleagues may make it difficult for you at first. After all, the idea that you might change your life while they stick to the same old path may be hugely uncomfortable for them. Humans are creatures of habit and we don't like someone upsetting the apple cart.

That's when you have to remember that you're fulfilling one of the most significant of all obligations – the one to yourself. If you are self-focused, people will realise that you have the courage and determination to do what you have set your mind on and their objections will gradually fade away. They'll come to see you as someone to admire, a role model for positive action and someone from whom they can learn. Meanwhile, in your temporary absence, your family will learn to cook, your best friend will get off the sofa and your work mates will probably still be at the same place drinking when you complete your triathlon.

MAKE SPACE FOR YOUR DREAMS

How often have you used your children, your work or even the weather as an excuse for putting things off? I know we live in busy and challenging times, but unless you're Sleeping Beauty, the job, person or object of your dreams isn't going to come knocking on the door. You have to make space for what you want and show yourself and others that you are serious. I'm a firm believer in the maxim 'if you don't ask, you don't get', and you can't ask for something if you haven't positively made room for it in your life.

So how do you do that? First, you need to clear a place in your head so that every time you think about your goal or dream, you don't just see a velvet rope and a sign that says, 'House Full'. In that special space you, and only you, are the VIP. Try to visit that space at the same time each day to dream, make concrete plans or just have restful thoughts. If you have to change your physical environment – by sitting in a café or whatever – then do it. It's all down to taking control and that all-important self-focus. You'll be surprised how good you feel when you've taken that relatively small step. Just thinking about it will help to make it real.

Now take it to the next level. I'm a great fan of the 'ideal day' exercise in which you create a picture of your perfect day from the moment you wake up in the morning until you go to sleep at night. Are you outdoors or indoors? Are you by the sea or in the mountains? What is your ideal view? What would you eat? Who would you be? This really is a wonderful way to tap into what you really want. And the best part is, nobody else will have the same day. It's uniquely yours. Just as you own that 'ideal day', so too can you take ownership of your dreams and desires.

LIVE IN THE PRESENT

One of the most difficult challenges in adopting a positive attitude is to avoid constant references to things that have occurred in the past. I'm not talking about tragedies or bereavements that require time to heal but those thoughts that start something like, 'If only I'd gone to university, married my childhood sweetheart, had children, never left that job…' Does that sound familiar?

It is wholly understandable that, for example, reflecting upon relationships that have ended can be hugely painful. So I really think you have to ask yourself whether it is helpful to soak yourself in the past, rather than learning from the experience and then going forward and creating new opportunities. The happy divorcee is undoubtedly going to find a fresh, new, exciting relationship much faster than the bitter ex-spouse who is continually looking backwards. The business man who is forever dwelling on the millions he just missed out on will never rise again and make the fortune he originally dreamed of.

Dwelling on the past can take up an awful lot of time and make you deeply unhappy. Don't get me wrong, I fully understand the temptation to do it. But what's the point? Yesterday is history. Tomorrow hasn't happened. That leaves today. That's all you have.

- ★ **The only life that matters is the one you're living now.**
- ★ **It's the only thing you should be focused on.**

You can't control the past so there is absolutely no reason why you should beat yourself up about it. If you find you keep torturing yourself with past memories, then I recommend you do the following exercise:

- ★ **Take all those feelings of guilt, regret, shame, recrimination, anger, frustration and sadness and write them down. You don't have to list them all at once; you can write them down when they each occur to you.**
- ★ **When you have written them down, fold up the paper and put it in an envelope. Now seal it. Then burn it. If that sounds too momentous, shred it. Or bury it somewhere.**
- ★ **Now your past is gone. You can't dig it up. You can't do anything about it. You have to get on with the present.**

And you know what? While the negative person has just read this suggestion and gone 'bah humbug', the positive person will do it, maybe reluctantly, but they'll do it, because they'll think, 'Hey! What have I got to lose? It might just work!'

The ability to live in the here and now is one of the secrets of true happiness. Just watch children playing and observe their utter concentration on what they're doing at that very moment. Whether it's pushing a toy truck or trying to fit some Lego together, they're totally immersed in the task. There is no 'next' for them because all they know about is the 'now'. One of the problems with being an adult (and there are many) is that we take things for granted. Years of living have tended to diminish our ability to be surprised and instead we become creatures of habit, no longer taking pleasure in our moments.

A toddler's delight in seeing snow or the seaside for the first time is a wonderful thing to behold. Young children seem to extract so much joy from the moment and their joy is contagious. You can experience the same pleasures too. I'm not suggesting you go rolling down a hill (although I do recall it being fun!). Simply revel in your own moments. Acknowledge the things that you normally take for granted. Slow down and enjoy the taste of a glass of wine, rather than guzzling it. Make an effort to look at the architecture around you as you go on your usual daily walk. Admire the evening light, or just sit with your mum in her garden and think, 'Gosh!

It feels good to do this.' After all, this could be the last time you'll have this moment.

SMALL STEPS TO THE STARS

For more than 30 years, I've operated in a world in which there is no such thing as a set career path. Instead, stepping stones emerge, a bit like *Takeshi's Castle* – that ludicrous game show on satellite TV, where contestants try to cross a lake hopping from one semi-submerged mushroom to another, trying to choose the one that will put them on a sure footing. I set off down the route of being 'Noel on Radio Luxembourg' without having a major plan. Sure, I dreamed of being on Radio One, but all the opportunities that came along afterwards happened, I believe, because I had focused on doing the first thing as well as I could. I didn't for one moment think where I was going next, largely because I had so much to learn and I was utterly obsessed with the radio environment. I just lived from day to day and tried to make the most of each step I took.

By concentrating on the moment in hand, I did the job better than I would have if I'd constantly worried about the next five years. (I know that one of the questions many employers like to ask is, 'Where do you see yourself in five years' time?' My response to that would be, 'Well, if I focus on what I'm doing now rather than worrying about the future, I'll hopefully have a choice of opportunities when I get there.')

While aiming for the stars may be your ultimate goal, you'll need to take more modest steps initially to help you to get there. People who manage to get things done generally do so because they set realistic interim targets that they know can be achieved. They don't get ahead of themselves. They set small goals that can be reached easily and, once they've managed those, they then set slightly harder ones. They don't sabotage their long-term aims by setting impossible goals, for example, saying they're going to play the piano as well as they did 15 years ago, or they will lose five kilos in a week. If you do that, every task becomes too big and unmanageable. It also gives you an excuse to accept failure and say inaccurate things like, 'Well it was too hard for me anyway.'

Let's say you want a special holiday – maybe you dream of going on safari in Africa. Meanwhile you continue to live the life you'd been living before you decided on your goal. You still spend several pounds a day on coffee at your favourite café, money you could be putting towards the safari. Keep doing that and you'll just sabotage your plan. If you really want to walk with the animals then you need to do something positive towards achieving it. I'm sorry, but just wanting it is not enough. You have to *show* that you want it – and that means taking action.

Geldof – the man who breaks all the rules

There will always be some people who prove to be the exception to the rule. One of the most exceptional people I can think of is Bob Geldof. Incredibly positive in his outlook, he approached the *Live Aid* project with what I can only describe as maniacal focus. No small steps for him. This was a project that demanded seriously big thinking. You know the rest of the story, but it was amazing to be just one tiny part of it.

In the 1980s, along with my partner Ged Hughes, I ran a helicopter business from Battersea Heliport in London. We'd only been in existence for a short time when we got a phone call from Bob Geldof, who was organising a pop concert in aid of the millions starving in Africa. That really is how most people in the business found out about *Live Aid*, by being told, 'Bob's putting together some pop acts and hopes to get Wembley and link it to a site in Philadelphia.' If positivity has a human form, it is undoubtedly Bob Geldof.

Bob had been told by the concert organiser, Harvey Goldsmith, that if all the artists brought all their friends and back-up team at the same time there would be something like 4,000 people back stage – clearly a totally impossible situation. The answer was to 'shuttle' the artists into Wembley shortly before their allotted performance time. Bob made it quite clear he needed helicopters and that the whole thing had to work meticulously. It was a logistical nightmare but, like everyone else, we wanted to do it for Bob.

What if pilots went sick? What if one of the big twin-engined craft had a technical fault? What if there were problems with London Air Traffic Control? What if… ? What if… ? What if… ? In the end, we all agreed that if it was going to work it would probably be because of some sort of divine intervention as much as our own efforts. And of course, work it did. After the trials and tribulations of getting consent to land alongside Concorde, it was a complete shock when Heathrow Air Traffic Control actually cleared us for an approach down the main active runway. As we taxied alongside the world's most iconic aircraft and delivered Phil Collins to Concorde, I had tears in my eyes.

Ours was a tiny contribution to an event that will forever be 'Geldof's finest hour'. He demonstrated what unstinting focus and belief (and sheer stubbornness) could accomplish. He set out a marker to show what one man could achieve if he set his mind to it. What a positive force he was, and how grateful I am that he made that phone call.

KEEPING IT TOGETHER (WHILE THE HOUSE IS FALLING DOWN)

Sometimes, despite all our efforts, we are not in control of our fate. *Noel's House Party* began in 1990 and for the first five years was an immense success. At its peak, the show pulled in audience figures of 17 million and both the show and I won many awards. In 1995 I was offered a new contract by the BBC, guaranteeing a further four years with the show.

This contract made me the highest paid entertainer

on TV. This period also coincided with what I consider to be my worst years at the BBC, when creative people suddenly found themselves at the mercy of an army of management consultants. Some people outside the industry may think I'm exaggerating when I say that those people wreaked havoc on the BBC's culture and philosophy, but I'd never seen programme makers dominated by accountants before – and that was a seriously major shift for someone who'd been in the business as long as I had by then.

The changes meant that a lot of talented people – both on- and off-screen – departed during the late 1990s. Morale went through the floor as many BBC services were outsourced. This included security, catering and even the financial department. (We used to go to Shepherd's Bush market to buy music tracks because it was cheaper than hiring them from the BBC's own record library!)

The move towards hiring freelancers rather than permanent staff meant there was little continuity in the entertainment department. Each year we had a brand new team, a situation that ensured that it often took many months for the personalities of all the members of the team to gel. In one series this never happened.

As the flagship light entertainment show, *House Party* was particularly badly affected by the new culture. Our programme budgets were cut 15 per cent year on year. As a consequence, we were not able to produce the innovative entertainment for which we'd been recognised in the past. We knew it wasn't up to the standards we'd set ourselves at the beginning and the audience reacted accordingly. No viewer sits at home thinking, 'My word, Noel's doing very well to continue to entertain us, bearing in mind the bloke has had his programme budget slashed.' They simply say, 'Well this stuff is not as good as it used to be.' And then they change channel. Friends have told me that when they watched the show, they could tell by the look in my eyes that I was desperately trying to make up for what we'd lost in terms of production values and content. It was hardly a recipe for light-hearted Saturday night entertainment.

Presenting *House Party* became a real strain and in the final year of the show I'd travel to work at BBC Television Centre with the heaviest of hearts. Years of enthusiasm seemed to have deserted me and the days when I couldn't believe the BBC actually paid me to have so much fun were now long gone. I was struggling just to keep my head above water.

The problems we were having generated a media (well, tabloid) feeding frenzy. It was a disappointing and demoralising time and there were many occasions when I would have loved to have quit. But I had a contract and a fierce sense of loyalty to Alan Yentob and the other executives who had supported me for so many years, which meant that I had to be professional and stay until the end. I knew I was doing the very best I could under the circumstances. If that wasn't good enough for others there was nothing more I could do about it.

PEOPLE ARE NOT BORN STRONG – THEY BECOME THAT WAY

At this point, I reckoned this particular chapter in my life was over. I know that I left 'Auntie BBC' on a low. I know that the media's perception is that I had an acrimonious departure after three decades with the BBC. But it so happens that I left the industry more on my terms than some people would wish to concede. I'd had 30 wonderful years, achieved a great deal in my chosen field and had been successful where many others had failed. I had enjoyed a wonderful bond with millions of listeners and viewers; thankfully a relationship that endures to this day. I also believe that everything has to end some time. I'd had a lot of success so, I suppose, if you look at it philosophically, it was my turn to take a fall. That's the way life goes sometimes and you can't fight it.

It wasn't a happy time but it wasn't devastating either. My life outside television wasn't as miserable as certain tabloid editors have made out. I don't know where people think TV personalities go to when they are not appearing on the small screen, but I can assure you that most of us are not sitting in an inner-city flat watching paint peeling off the walls and listening to leaking water drip into a bucket. There is life outside TV, just as there is life outside any job. I had my baby daughter to play with, something I never had time to do when my other children were young, and I made the most of that time. I had lots of other challenges and I knew my time in television would come again if it was meant to (more positive thinking). Sooner or later, everyone has a bad patch. While some people take it in their stride, there are others who fall to pieces at the first sign of adversity.

There is a school of thought that suggests some people are naturally 'strong' while others are not. Thus if something unfortunate happens the strong ones will get over it effortlessly while others will have a much harder time. I don't really buy that. I just think it's more the case that some people choose to see the rough patches as a part of their journey. That means not over analysing the situation or being hypercritical of themselves. Instead of hitting their heads against a brick wall by trying to figure out how it could have been different, they just accept that it has happened and try to learn from it. I think I learned a lot from my time away from television. As well as broadening my life generally, it also gave me something I didn't have while I was working in the business – namely the chance to see TV from another perspective.

Of course, if you have been sacked from your job, or the love of your life has left you, you're bound to indulge in a little self-pity. The problem comes when you use these setbacks as an excuse to let go of your self-focus – and your self-respect. One of the reasons why I have never taken drugs and, with very few exceptions, never drink to excess, is that I hate feeling I'm not in control. I know that many people love this sensation because it makes them feel free, but I become extremely unsettled, bordering on fearful, if I think I am not on top of the situation. We all have to find the level of self-control we're happy with. Too little, and we're in danger of losing our self-respect. Too much, and we're also in danger, but this time of becoming self-obsessed. I do think it's vital that when you are going through a difficult time you pay even more attention to your physical well-being than you would normally. Don't let the world see you crumble. Instead, get up, have a shower, put on your favourite clothes and remember that you're still the person you've always been. You've just had a setback, that's all.

WHEN YOU'RE COMFORTABLE IN YOUR SKIN IT SHOWS

Living in France for part of my time, I've had to immerse myself in a new language. The French have many wonderful expressions (some of which can't be translated literally). There is one that goes '*être bien dans sa peau*'. It means 'being happy in your skin'. This is something you see in all great sports stars. It's a combination of many things – confidence, skill, self-knowledge, a positive attitude. It's quite hard to put your finger on it. But the people who have it tend to make a huge impact, and not because they're noisy or showy. In fact, quite the opposite. They are self-contained and self-possessed.

In my motor racing days, I had some fantastic opportunities not only to race interesting cars but also to meet some of the most accomplished racing drivers of the modern era. You could not find a greater contrast than between Jackie Stewart and James Hunt. With James I competed in a three-day round-Britain motor rally in 1976, the same year that he was destined to win the British Grand Prix (although later disqualified) and the Formula One World Championship. The impression I formed of James was similar to that of many other people. A legendary womaniser, James could be pretty unpleasant to the fans, which was pretty embarrassing for me as our joint efforts were being heavily promoted by Radio One. I was uncomfortable with his boasting and his over-the-top aggressive attitude. Our attempt to win the Tour of Britain, which ended on day one with a spectacular crash, was probably doomed from the outset.

Contrast this with my experience of Jackie Stewart, a racing star who had dominated Formula One racing for so many years and who had made such a significant contribution to motor racing safety. Being driven around Silverstone Grand Prix circuit by Jackie was one of the highlights of my life. Everything was so effortless. In contrast to James Hunt's 'balls out' aggressive style, Jackie maintained a brilliant commentary even with the car in a full blown power slide at 150 mph. Despite the speeds we were travelling at, I never thought for one moment that anything could possibly go wrong. His confidence and talent were apparent to even the most terrified passenger. More to the point, Jackie Stewart *knew* that he was in control. His positive approach boosted his obvious physical and mental talents and left you in no doubt that here was a man truly 'happy in his skin'.

When you are in possession of yourself, you stop being reactive. Rather than constantly asking what other people think, you become secure enough to rely on yourself. Self-focused people are in it for the long haul. They are not easily distracted from their goal, nor do they let obstacles put them off.

Self-focus is not being obsessive, selfish or self-centered. It's about:

- **Taking responsibility for your own path to happiness.**
- **Actively claiming space and time for yourself and your dreams.**
- **Putting the past behind you and not letting it put you off your goals.**
- **Maintaining your self-respect in the face of adversity, and ultimately…**
- **… Being happy in your skin.**

CHAPTER 3

MEASURE YOU AGAINST YOU

ONE OF THE easiest ways to diminish your efforts in achieving a positive existence is to compare yourself with other people. I believe this is a major source of unhappiness and something that doesn't just affect us individually but our collective well-being as well. Think about it. If everyone is looking around wishing they were someone else, there's not going to be a lot of happiness and contentment in evidence. When we constantly compare ourselves and our lives with others, we make it harder to accept ourselves and achieve what we are capable of. The move towards self-acceptance is one of the most positive and utterly liberating moves you can make in your life.

Do any of the statements overleaf sound familiar?

- ★ **You get irritable or upset when something good happens to someone else.**
- ★ **If you meet a successful, happy person, you feel that your importance as a human being is diminished.**
- ★ **You knock others and hope they'll fail.**
- ★ **You don't take compliments gracefully and never feel you are good enough.**
- ★ **Your happy moments fade away really quickly.**

If any of them do, then you're probably the kind of person who constantly compares yourself with others, and you find it hard to accept yourself as you are. We all have strengths, weaknesses, limitations and abilities. The best thing you can do for yourself in this life is to strive to make the most of what you have. The worst thing you can do is waste energy making fruitless comparisons. I want to draw a distinction here between a brief moment spent admiring or appreciating somebody – which is perfectly healthy – and devoting a great deal of time to wishing you were that person – which is unhealthy. Why would you do it?

I'll be the first to admit that the media doesn't help us to accept ourselves, particularly when it comes to physical appearance. There are now so many magazines and TV programmes devoted to telling us how to look and how to live and bombarding us with the fabulous lives of the rich and famous that it's pretty hard to ignore. As the father of four daughters, I'm well aware of the media's influence. Thankfully, my girls know that those so-called perfect-looking women are the beneficiaries of the efforts of nutritionists, stylists, hairdressers, makeup artists, personal trainers, life coaches and a whole host of other experts who make sure they're absolutely up to scratch. And they devote their whole lives – and substantial amounts of cash – to maintaining that look and that lifestyle.

If three hours of dedication a day doesn't work, their photographic images in magazines and newspapers can be enhanced by computer programmes whose ability to remove lines and fat, add cheekbones and change eye colour knows no bounds. Please remember that, the next time you look at a magazine. And remember, too, that the job of magazine editors is to sell more magazines. I'm now going to let you in on a little secret. It's a well-established fact that if you list, say, 'The 100 Most Beautiful Women' (or 'The 50 Most Eligible Bachelors', or whatever) on the cover you will sell thousands more magazines than if you show something else. It's not that these '100 Most Beautiful Women' represent the ultimate definition of feminine perfection – they are simply ideals that reflect the period we're living in. Or more likely, they reflect the need of the features editor to fill some space and their knowledge that certain types of article will always sell. Think about it logically. How could they possibly have selected just 100 women from the millions of beautiful women in the world? It's just a business. As I always say, we get the media we deserve. But that is a whole other story.

It's not just women who compare themselves with others. I have to admit that on meeting some of the university students who travel from all over Britain to be in the audience of *Deal or No Deal*, I have often thought how great it would be to be a carefree, broad-shouldered, six-foot three-inch surfer boy. What bloke wouldn't? But I don't spend time feeling miserable about it. At least with physical comparisons you can always dismiss another's looks as a piece of genetic good fortune. The science bit is always easier to explain away. But what do you do about those other comparisons that have to do with success, status and emotional well-being?

ANOTHER PERSON'S GAIN IS NOT YOUR LOSS

How do you react when a colleague receives a coveted promotion ahead of you, your mate meets the love of his life, or your best friend gets pregnant (despite the fact that you've been trying to conceive for much longer)? Well, if you're like most people, it's possible you'll feel envious/angry/frustrated/cheated or the whole lot rolled into one. One way of looking at it is that someone else has got what was rightfully ours. However, if you can manage to see past the emotions of the moment, you'll realise that is not the case.

Just because good fortune has smiled upon somebody

else, it doesn't mean that you have lost anything. You're still where you were before. What happened to a friend or colleague had nothing to do with you – even if, for example, you applied for the same promotion. It simply means that the cosmos decided it was their turn, not yours. No one has taken anything from you personally. You don't have any less than you had before and there is still every chance that, in time, you will have the 'luck' you desire. You may find that it was a blessing not getting the promotion then and you are able to take advantage of a better opportunity later on. We all have our moments, and as long as we focus our efforts on what we truly want, something good will come of it. One door may close but another one will open – you may just have to wait. However, if we choose to focus on what others have, we will diminish our own chances of happiness.

Of course, there are times when life just isn't fair. But who said it was? In the first chapter I talked about not labelling yourself as the 'unlucky' one. But remember there is a difference between luck and fortune. You really do have influence over how fortunate you are. I would now add that it doesn't help to dwell continually on the fact that life is unfair towards you. There are people who are probably a lot more deserving of a break than you or me but do they get a chance? Accept that luck is incapable of distinguishing the deserving from the non-deserving and make sure that all your dealings in life are as fair as they can be.

Meanwhile, you have to get yourself out of the mindset that there is such a thing as a perfect life. Having met people who most would consider had fabulous lifestyles, I can categorically state that appearances can be deceptive. My own lifestyle – a beautiful wife, four lovely daughters, a country house and a great career – is just one example of this but everyone's life involves trade-offs. The beautiful woman at the party has an eating disorder because she believes men only want her for her looks. The man with the high-flying job feels sick everyday and wishes he had the courage to resign and travel the world. The woman who marries the wealthy executive may get a beautiful house and a big bank account but how much time does her husband spend with her?

By the way, as much as I enjoy the freedom that money gives me, I also know that money cannot be a substitute for emotional happiness. My girls are very much my focus and it is great to be able to do wonderful things for them, but the love we share is far more important. A big bank account will not compensate for deficiencies in your emotional life. (If it did, lots of people would be content to sit and count their money, instead of being hugged.)

Let's talk for a minute about those people with whom you compare yourself. Do you honestly think they're happy with who they are? I'm not saying this to make you feel better but just to remind you that everyone is striving. Actually that's not true. The really lucky few are ambling, or perhaps skipping, but, yes, everyone is looking for a place in the world. And I'm sure some of the people you compare yourself with would hate to think of themselves as role models. They probably think you have it all.

Consider this, too. If you had 'It' (whatever 'It' might be) would you be happy? My bet is that you wouldn't. You will only be truly satisfied when you find your place in the world. That is the place where your skills, ability, personality and dreams all come together. We may all be made out of the same cookie dough but we are all individuals. It's only when you tap into your true self that you will be happy. Doing that means accepting yourself and discovering those special qualities that make you YOU.

Start by writing down 10 positive words to describe yourself. Write them on a card – the size of a business card will do – and bring it out whenever you feel insecure or your self-esteem is running low. Bring it out before you walk into a big party or go to an important meeting. It will help you, believe me. Carry it everywhere.

NOBODY IS GOOD AT EVERYTHING

Working as I do in 'TV land', it's just too easy to fall into the trap of looking around you and comparing your abilities with those who surround you. I think one of the reasons I've managed to have a long career in broadcasting is that I've understood my strengths and weaknesses and chosen my career opportunities accordingly. I've declined a lot of fantastic opportunities during my career and in recent years said 'no' to offers that just didn't excite me. Now that *DoND* is such a huge success I am really pleased I did decline some of the suggestions that were put my way over the past six years. I've been able to return fresh and with renewed energy. I can't sing and I can't dance. On a good day (probably assisted by Chardonnay) I can tell the odd good joke. Yet I have been able to find my own niche in television. This is particularly true of the *Noel's House Party* years and now *DoND*, where I believe I have finally found the format that sits most comfortably with my own personality and style of presenting. The role I play on *DoND* is the closest to me. For reasons that I cannot quantify and certainly don't want to analyse too deeply, I am able to strike a chord with people through television and, particularly, this programme – and I am truly grateful for it.

That doesn't mean there aren't days when I wish I'd had the comic genius of Kenny Everett (who doesn't?) or, in terms of contemporary radio, the lyrical touch of Terry Wogan or the wit of Jonathan Ross. But I also know that it is rare for anyone to be good at both radio and television. Two radio heroes of mine, John Peel and Tony Blackburn, have both worked in television but I'm not sure it has ever lived up to radio. Chris Tarrant has been highly successful on both TV and radio but he, too, is an exception rather than the rule.

If you think about successful light entertainment programmes, one of the reasons they work is that the right people are doing the job. I absolutely loved presenting *Top Gear* all those years ago, but as an avid viewer of today's production, I have to recognise that the efforts of Messrs Hammond, May and Clarkson totally eclipse my own. Then there is the sheer brilliance of Paul Merton on *Have I Got News For You* and that bubbly and brilliant duo Ant and Dec. All are very comfortable with the formats they work in, so the programmes do not seem contrived or forced, which would be the case if the wrong people were at the helm.

All actors have favourite roles in which they feel most at ease. These are often roles that tap into something deep in their personality; an extension of their own character. It's the same in the sporting world. A footballer may be unsuccessful at one club and yet may thrive at another simply because it is a better 'fit' with him. Even though I loved working with the team at Pebble Mill when I presented *Telly Addicts*, and the show ran for 13 years, it was never my most comfortable 'role'. However, there were aspects of the show that I totally enjoyed, such as interacting with the members of the public who were playing the game. It was great fun doing the show, but it certainly wasn't my finest hour. Likewise, the recorded and heavily edited *Saturday Road Show* wasn't the enormous challenge that was subsequently provided by *House Party*. I loved presenting all of these shows, but the biggest successes were those that created the perfect fit with the real me.

They made it their own

Tonight was a hugely influential current affairs programme that was on television during my teenage years. It fostered the talents of some of our most brilliant broadcasters and producers. My particular favourite was Alan Whicker, who went on to make a whole genre of broadcasting – the TV travelogue – very much his own. Our paths didn't cross until BBC One invited me to host the BAFTA Awards Ceremony live from Grosvenor House in London. In those days, the ceremony comprised a room full of film luvvies and television grafters whose mutual enmity was tangible. Add a royal guest and a top table of industry types, and making one mistake at this gig could have had a fundamental – and terminal – effect on my career. If I was ever going to suffer nerves before a live broadcast, this was the occasion. As I waited to be cued on by the floor manager, the first award presenter appeared alongside me – my hero Alan Whicker. I exchanged pleasantries with him while thinking of the ordeal ahead. Imagine my surprise, and then almost instantaneous utter relief, to see that his hands were shaking so much he couldn't read the category name on the outside of the gold envelope. My hero was a human being too.

Undoubtedly, one of the greatest performers I have ever had the privilege of working with was Bob Monkhouse. Like me, he attracted his fair share of negative publicity. He, too, knew the ups and downs of the profession. But he was the consummate professional. Nobody, but nobody, worked a live studio audience – or a sales conference – better than Bob

Monkhouse. His comedic delivery was impeccable. His rapport with the audience was total. Film star, singer, gag writer for Bob Hope, quiz master, game show host and brilliant stand-up, he was the ultimate all-round entertainer.

BE PROUD OF YOUR ACCOMPLISHMENTS

Possibly the greatest compliment I've received during my broadcasting career is that I 'make live television look easy'. Deep down, I know just how hard I'm working and that I can't afford to relax too much. These days, I have the best, young, enthusiastic production team in Bristol – all of them a joy to work with. I never forget how much I depend on their efforts before I can begin putting in my own. Finally, I love what I do so, naturally, I want to find ways of getting even better at it. The only person I compare myself with is me, and since we record 30 shows in a block, there's a lot of 'me' with which to compare. I accept that there are days when, because of the attitude of the contestants, the vibes in the studio and, yes, the cosmos, everything comes together in an almost perfect way. (And, of course, there are days when I have to dig really deep to make it happen.)

But remember, as I've already pointed out, there is no such thing as a universal definition of what makes the perfect job, perfect performance, perfect relationship or even the perfect beach. Like beauty, perfection is in the eye of the beholder. Just as you don't necessarily blindly accept a critic's view of a film or a book but choose to read it for yourself, so you don't need to accept attempts by the media, friends, colleagues or whoever to make you conform to a collective view of 'the perfect life'. Make your own. Experiment. Learn. And take pride in what you do.

If you've accepted the premise of this book – and if you've read this far – then I assume you want to change your behaviour. The first thing you need to do is acknowledge your strengths.

Write down 10 things about yourself that you feel good about. Things like:

★ **I am kind to others.**
★ **I have a great memory.**
★ **My golf swing is pretty good.**
★ **Everybody loves my cooking.**
★ **I rewired the whole house.**
★ **Children and animals love me.**

These may not sound huge to you but they are the kind of achievements that make up most people's lives. The lives of at least 99 per cent of us, in fact. There is only a minuscule handful of people in the world who can lay claim to the stuff that changes lives and makes history. The rest – well, we're all in pretty much the same boat. Make sure you look at this list regularly. I recommend you take it with you wherever you go. Use it like a set of affirmations to remind yourself of what you can do. Every month add one new thing to the list. Pretty soon you'll have quite an impressive collection of achievements that are unique to you. They are what make you who you are. Enjoy them.

PLAY TO YOUR STRENGTHS

I was offered the job of presenting *This is Your Life* when the late, great Eammon Andrews died. But I declined it. In part, this was because I did not feel comfortable doing it in the light of the fact that the previous presenter had died. In addition, I felt that the format was already so powerful there was nothing new I could bring to the party.

Right now I've got what, for me, is the hottest ticket in television. *DoND* is a presentation role that suits my character perfectly. There's loads of repartee with contestants – plus the opportunity to create and participate in the tension and drama. While I recognise that there are many more talented broadcasters than myself, I also recognise my ability to connect with the people in the studio and the viewers at home. I have been able to make the show mine and it's a good feeling to be in the right position. I had to think hard before returning to television and I am glad that the faith of Channel 4 and the production company Endemol has been vindicated.

I knew that *DoND* would be a success because it had already been sold to more than 40 countries world-wide. So there was no way it was going to fail with a British audience. But I wondered how I would be received by members of the public who already knew me, as well as a whole new audience who were just babies or toddlers when I left the BBC. It matters a lot to me that the show has done brilliantly. I am very proud of the programme, the crew and, yes, myself. And I think the reason it has worked for me is that I chose the right 'fit'. The show plays to my strengths and yet enables me to stretch myself as well.

I'm enormously grateful that Adam Macdonald and Kevin Lygo at Channel 4 and Peter Bazalgette at Endemol worked so hard to persuade me that my initial decision to decline their offer was wrong. I will never forget sitting in the production office in Shepherds Bush talking the show through with producers Richard Hague, Glen Hugill and Stephen Boodhun and the format creator Dick de Rijk. We gelled immediately, and as I played the game and Glen performed the role that was to become me, I finally realised that this really was the show to warrant my coming back to television.

When something fits you well – whether it's a job or relationship – you'll find that you don't have to contrive to make it work. It's not a case of needing to make less effort. It's more that the effort you put in is rewarded in spades because you've found the right place for you, rather than trying to squeeze yourself into something that clearly wasn't meant for you. If, for example, your character is such that money is the absolute prime motivator, then you might be happy to change your job purely for financial gain. On the other hand, if you're somebody who values freedom and taking a new job would mean being answerable to a very controlling boss, then it is likely that no amount of money in the world is going to make it the right 'fit' for you.

It's factors like these that render comparisons meaningless. There is no rule book that says you have to take the job that offers the most money. It's always heartening to see bright young graduates, who might otherwise have gone into the City, choosing to become teachers because they genuinely want to make a difference. For them, the cut and thrust of the financial world is a stretch too far – even if the financial rewards are huge. These young people have recognised that they need to find the right place, not just for their skills but also for their emotional needs. As I said at the beginning of this chapter, there are trade-offs with everything. The trick is to play with the pieces of your own personal life jigsaw until they come together in a way that suits you and shows you at your best.

BE THE BEST YOU CAN BE

It doesn't matter whether you're a teacher, a cleaner, an accountant or a plumber. You owe it to yourself to do each task as well as it can possibly be done. One of the phrases I least like hearing is, 'Oh, it will do.' It might not immediately strike you as being a negative expression but it is. There is a kind of resignation implicit in it, like saying, 'That is all I can do.' When I was restoring the magnificent Broomford Estate in Devon, I had the good fortune to have as my estate manager a man called Gordon Reynolds. He was one of the most accomplished and charismatic individuals I have ever met. Whenever we were working on a task, Gordon would use the expression, 'That's a Broomford job', meaning no corners had been cut and the finished result would stand the test of time. I feel that way about everything I do, and I must admit that I sometimes walk a fine line between not accepting what I've done and trying to motivate myself to do even better.

House Party might have looked like lots of disorganised fun but I had a very carefully worked out routine for the build-up to the show. On a Friday morning, I would travel up to London, usually by car, and spend the rest of the day with the production team running through every detail of that week's show. By 7 pm on Friday, 90 per cent of the show was in place. I then went back to the hotel I always stayed at, located a few minutes away in Holland Park. I'd then set about learning every single sketch and the entire running order. I presented *House Party* without an ear piece and without using an autocue, so I had to commit everything to memory – all 50 minutes of it.

I was always in bed by 9 pm and invariably watched *Cheers* before blocking out the world with earplugs and turning out the light. Next morning, I would start memorising everything all over again. By lunch time I was at the Television Centre and on the stroke of 2 pm we would do the first run-through of the show to cameras. The dress rehearsal would begin at 4 pm, and then there was usually a 30-minute gap before we went live. By now, I was so familiar with the show's content that any nerves I might have felt just evaporated. When the show was over, it was back to the dressing room to remove my makeup and reflect on the show. Because I am very self-critical, no show was ever perfect. The producer, Michael Leggo, and I would have a brief conversation about the events of the last hour and then I would walk out, climb into my car and drive the 250 miles home to Devon, hopefully with the satisfaction of having done the job as well as I could. And that is the best you can ask of yourself.

ENJOY WHAT YOU HAVE ALREADY ACHIEVED

As a boy, I had a permanent model railway installed around the walls of my bedroom. I say 'permanent' but the reality was that I was forever changing it. This was because I was constantly trying to improve it. I make this point because, later on in life, I recall my father saying to me on a number of occasions that I was 'never satisfied'. His comments would invariably follow the purchase of another new car or ambitious plans for an extension to my new home. For all his strengths, my Dad often interpreted my quest for moving ahead in my life as being a sign of some deep-rooted dissatisfaction. I now realise I was actually just being extraordinarily positive. Positive individuals are always seeking some improvement to their current status, whether financial, spiritual, emotional or physical. Positive individuals will always demand more out of life. I don't think there is anything wrong with being like that, so long as you do it for the right reasons and you're not constantly asking, 'Is that all there is?' That means that your happiness shouldn't be dependent on getting 'more' and, first and foremost, you should be grateful for what you have and not take it for granted.

Early on in this book I talked about living in the present as a way of focusing your mind. Elsewhere I've also spoken about the need to slow down and enjoy the 'moments' and not take life for granted. Sometimes it is all too easy to forget that we have one life – the one we're living now – and that means appreciating what you have achieved already in that life. Don't get ahead of yourself. How often have you started talking about next year's holiday while you're in the middle of this year's? It's not really a recipe for making the most of what you have, is it? Being grateful for what you have achieved is an exercise in self-acceptance as well. Life won't begin when you get a new car, lose some weight or take early retirement. It's happening now.

When you accept yourself for the unique person you are, you'll notice the positive aspects of yourself and you'll be less likely to spend time judging and evaluating yourself.

The only person you should ever measure yourself against is you. Instead of comparing yourself to others you should:

- ★ Accept there is no such thing as a perfect life, job or relationship.
- ★ Remember that someone else's good fortune is not your bad fortune.
- ★ Remember that you are a unique individual with your own set of achievements.
- ★ Focus on what you can do well and not what you do badly.
- ★ Accept that you don't have to live up to anyone else's standards – set your own.
- ★ Be grateful for what you have achieved so far and remember that the life you're living now is the real one.

CHAPTER 4

BE A PART OF THE WORLD

I READ A SHORT ARTICLE in the *Guardian* that should really have been a much longer article. It said that half the UK population avoids making small talk with strangers. The strangers in question were not shadowy figures on street corners but customers in local shops, fellow parents at the school gates and neighbours whom the respondents admitted they did not know by name. While not surprising, I found this extremely sad.

Being afraid of other people is really being afraid of yourself. When you close yourself off from others, for whatever reason, you're giving up the opportunity to discover more about what makes you tick. People who make an effort to engage with others – whether by talking to their neighbours, being part of the local community or getting involved in the wider world through charity work – expose themselves to a wide range of positive experiences that can lead to greater happiness for others and add a wonderful dimension to their own lives. As economist Richard Layard puts it in his book *Happiness, Lessons From A New Science*: 'People who care about other people are on average happier than those who are more preoccupied with themselves.'

LISTEN AND YOU WILL BE HEARD

I want to talk about listening because I believe it's at the heart of many of our problems. Most of us are less interested in listening to others than in making ourselves heard. We go to great lengths in trying to make our point but don't really listen properly to what is being said. In fact, it's only when you spend time trying to understand someone and finding out what matters to them that you will find it easier to be understood yourself.

The point at which most relationships finally come to an end is usually a culmination of months or years of mini relationship breakdowns. In each case there will be many different factors involved but you can bet that, somewhere along the way, the individuals involved stopped listening to one another and one of them said, 'I don't want to talk about it any more.' Yes, it often is that simple.

Really listening means putting yourself to one side. It requires enormous self-discipline and self-control and the ability to suppress your desire to interrupt people. It's not enough to listen: you have to *show* the other person you are listening to them. That means focusing completely on what they're saying and not waiting for a break to jump in. Some people call this 'active listening'. It's very, very hard to do – especially in a world in which we constantly feel we have to do 20 things at once. But that doesn't mean you shouldn't try.

If you make an effort to understand others first, it enables you to get to the core of real issues far more quickly. That gives you a better chance of saying the right thing in reply. Giving space to the other person's words and feelings actually takes far less effort than trying to hit them over the head (not literally of course!) with your own point of view all the time. It's something that we're all guilty of doing.

Maybe it's all to do with our much-discussed hectic pace of life. Perhaps it's that we live in a world with so many distractions that conversation has been devalued and all that matters is getting our voice heard as rapidly as possible. Whatever it is, our personal interactions are now given as much importance as fast food. Is it any surprise that so many people are lonely?

Let me ask you this: when your children come into the room to speak to you, do you put down the newspaper or stop watching the television and pay attention to them? If you're like most people, you probably don't, which means you're not listening properly. But what sort of message are you sending out? You are effectively telling your children, 'Even you are not important enough for me to stop doing what I'm doing.' From the moment they are born, children are compelled to listen to others imposing views and ideas on them. If you're too busy talking to listen to your children and acknowledge their contribution, it's likely they will feel they are not worth the time and effort. So please listen and show that you are listening.

DON'T HIDE BEHIND TECHNOLOGY

In 2005, the International Grammar School, a private school in New South Wales, Australia, took the unusual step of banning its pupils from listening to their iPods. When asked why, the principal, Kerrie Murphy, replied that this practice isolated the kids from the rest of the world and encouraged them to be selfish and lonely. The children 'were not tuning into other people because they were tuned into themselves'. I think she has a point. I'm a huge fan of technology, in as far as it makes it possible for me to do all the things I need to do efficiently, but I worry that people use it as a substitute for face-to-face interaction, and that this forms a barrier between them and the world. For the notoriously distant Brit who is unable to interact with his/her fellow human, technology has become a new best friend.

How often do you send emails at work when you could as easily walk over to someone's desk and say what you need to say – and get an immediate response in the process? I'm as guilty as the next person of making and receiving far too many calls on my mobile, but I do try to be thoughtful when I'm with my family and friends. I find it really irritating when I see couples in restaurants who are not talking to each another but are playing with their mobiles instead. I think it is rather ludicrous how nowadays a group of people on an outing often do not communicate with their fellow passengers but talk into their phones instead. I say this as the person who made the first mobile phone call live on the BBC. (It didn't connect!)

Unless you are the person chosen to save the world that day, you really don't need to have your mobile on all the time. If nothing else, it smacks of bad manners. What is more important? Taking a phone call or actually enjoying the companionship of the people you're with? Mobiles have become our security blanket. They are a way of showing others that you are wanted (even if it's just a reminder about a dental appointment). The fact is that if you spent less time hugging the phone and more time hugging others you really would become that 'wanted' person you wish to be. Everyone wants to be with someone who is totally focused on them. Giving someone your full attention is incredibly attractive. If you think it's far more interesting to play with your mobile phone than talk to your date, don't be surprised if they leave you to your own devices.

DO SOMETHING FOR SOMEBODY YOU'VE NEVER MET

You might have heard the phrase 'random acts of kindness'. No one's sure exactly where the concept started but suffice to say that it seems to have come from the United States. One well-documented incident involved motorists on San Francisco's Golden Gate Bridge, each of whom paid the toll of the car behind them. The concept was that you would give a stranger something without expecting anything in return. It is a beautiful, simple idea that rests on the notion of being kind to a fellow human being you don't necessarily know.

One of the greatest advances you can make on your journey towards a more positive lifestyle is to ensure that you try to do something for someone else every single day. That might mean spending a significant amount of time doing voluntary work, or it could be as simple as saying 'Hello' to the pensioner who lives on her own, next time you pass her in the street. Or you might ask the girl in the post office how her day is going. I guarantee that it will make a huge difference to the person you speak to, and you will feel much better for it too. (I hate it when people walk past the same person every day and, instead of acknowledging them in some way, just puts their head down and ignores them.)

I'm not suggesting you adopt the American mantra of 'Have a nice day.' I just think that if simple pleasantries could be brought back into our daily lives it would make everyone feel a whole lot better. I love that aspect of France when I'm over there. You go into, say, the bakery, for a baguette or whatever, and there is this ritual they have where everyone says '*Bonjour*' when they enter and then '*Au revoir*' when they leave. It makes me feel delightfully civilised and it's certainly better than muttering under your breath or saying nothing at all.

When you connect with people in this way, the positive feelings you generate will be huge in proportion to this simple act of kindness. Imagine the change in the atmosphere if everyone in your street decided to do something kind for others. Plus, as you pull up the duvet and turn off the light at the end of yet another day, it's no bad thing to ask yourself the question, 'Did I make anybody's life a little bit more positive today?'

There are very few people in the UK who couldn't afford to give some of their money to a worthy cause. For example, there are some excellent schemes whereby you give a few pence a day to support children in Third World countries and it really does make a difference to them. Last Christmas, as an extra gift to my girls, I enrolled each of them in one of these schemes. It has undoubtedly made them more appreciative of what they have and it has also opened their eyes to what is going on in our world. As Chair of the NSPCC's Caring for Children in Court Appeal, I've signed up to the society's patron scheme. That means I'm committed to giving a percentage of my income each month for the next 10 years to the NSPCC, which will ensure that those children who are called as witnesses (often in cases where they are also the victims) will receive the appropriate professional support. I appreciate that such giving may be beyond the resources of many people but I mention it here purely to demonstrate the principle.

Of course, the most positive contribution you can make to somebody else's life doesn't involve money but requires you to donate that most precious commodity of all – your time. Like many others in my industry, I regularly receive requests to attend charity functions and become a patron of charitable organisations, all of them worthy. But because I don't think there's a point in confusing motion with action and doing things on a superficial level, I've developed my own 'giving' strategy which, in broad terms, is about what I can give to my local community.

My involvement with Exeter Leukaemia Fund and support for Children's Hospice South West comes from my love of the West Country and my determination to make a difference to the quality of life in that region. It is fantastically satisfying to know that, simply by being associated with these organisations and giving them a little bit of my time, I'm making a contribution to their fundraising success. One interviewer once asked if I engaged in such charity ventures because, 'I felt the need to put something back.' My reply was that I wasn't aware that I'd stolen something in the first place.

I don't give my time to charity organisations to boost my own profile and I certainly don't do it because I feel guilty about my own professional success. I do it because I believe in community spirit. I believe that we reap what we sow and we all have an obligation to assist those less fortunate than ourselves. Some of our communities do not have, or have lost, important facilities such as a post office, shops, a library or a school. Over the years there has been a decline in voluntary work, something that traditionally has helped to support local services and activities and fostered community spirit.

All this means that people are becoming increasingly disconnected from one another and from society as a whole. I believe that, instead of concentrating on the negative consequences of such social isolation, such as teenage crime, the media in general should take a more positive approach and give more space to community campaigns. We all know the problems, but writing screaming headlines about them isn't going to help people feel better. However, on a positive note, I have noticed a huge increase in community involvement over the past year, particularly in terms of campaigns such as saving local shops from the impact of big business. The more we get involved, the more we can change things.

THE WORLD IS MOVED BY ORDINARY PEOPLE

If you look at the people who make things happen in our communities they do not appear to be out of the ordinary. They certainly don't have a golden halo around their head. They're just people going about their normal daily lives – until one day they become so passionate about a cause that they decide things must change. My involvement with the NSPCC means that I've been privileged to observe the work of a couple of dozen people, mostly women, who make up the NSPCC Young Witness Support teams.

To appreciate the scale of the problem they are tackling, you must first understand the UK's appalling track record on child abuse. Every week in England and Wales, one to two children, on average, die following cruelty at the hands of parents or carers. Think about it. At least 100 children every year are killed by someone they should be able to rely on and trust.

One consequence of this is that every year approximately 30,000 children are called to give evidence against people who have subjected them to dreadful acts of sexual and physical abuse. Less than 4 per cent of these poor children receive appropriate professional support when they are thrown into the judicial system. No wonder so many child witnesses say that the ordeal of appearing in court is worse than the abuse they suffered. Despite recommendations made in a report published 15 years ago, barristers are still allowed to pose intimate questions in open court to these vulnerable children, even asking them to point to parts of their body. While some judges allow children to give evidence via video link, this practice is not uniform. In addition, not all children are screened from the rest of the court, and so they often have to face the accused.

These children have already had enough to deal with. The positive approach to their predicament would be to put measures in place to protect them in court. Their plight could be greatly eased almost instantly if there was the will in high places. Over the past two years I've met lawyers, judges, police officers, cabinet ministers and politicians, as well as countless civil servants, in my capacity as chair of the NSPCC's Caring for Children in Court Appeal. I've attended discussions at the highest levels within the Home Office, Law Society, Bar Council and Crown Prosecution Service. Without exception, every individual I've met has agreed that the way we treat the majority of child witnesses is a national disgrace and that something must be done about it. Then he or she leaves the meeting and, in most cases, nothing is done. In the meantime, thousands of young lives are being wrecked forever.

While I can go back to my day job, the tireless members of the NSPCC Young Witness Support teams continue to work with these poor children, day in and day out. As you can guess, they're not in it for the money. Or the glory. They're in it because they believe things have to change. And they believe they can do it. That's what gives them the strength to fight on.

Most of the significant improvements in this life are not achieved by people in the public eye but by people who decided they were fed up with just getting angry and negative. So they decided to change things. And you can do it too. Let me give you two examples of how I have surprised myself and discovered how it's possible to take action that gets results.

I've never thought of myself as militant. However, during the foot and mouth outbreak in the West Country in 2001, I realised I had to do something. Along with many others, I had found myself caught up in the mass cull in which millions of healthy animals were being murdered simply because politicians and government officials didn't know how to deal with the crisis. I've never felt anger like it, and I simply could not ignore the animal and human tragedy that was unfolding all around me. Millions of healthy animals were being slaughtered under the most inhumane conditions. The bodies were piled 20 feet high in some places and the stench was unbelievable. So, in my little part of Devon, we mounted an active resistance to the killing machine. It was a small organisation called 'The Heart of Devon' that acted as an information line for the hundreds of farmers who were marooned in almost total ignorance on their farms.

I am certain that we were a real thorn in the side of the Ministry of Agriculture, Fisheries and Food (MAFF) officials and I'd like to think that we helped protect the livelihoods of hundreds of people in the affected areas. I know for a fact that Heart of Devon prevented seven major culls of perfectly healthy animals. My local MP pointed out to me that I probably now have my own file in some corner of Whitehall marking me as a 'subversive' and 'one to be watched'! Who'd have thought it?

POSITIVE PROTEST IS ESSENTIAL

When a local action group asked me to become involved in their fight against a planning application for giant wind turbines close to Dartmoor, I realised that I had to adopt a positive attitude and not simply be yet another negative protester. Indeed, this would be my advice to anybody fighting bureaucracy and undesirable planning decisions, whether it's wind farms, a by-pass, or whatever. Simply saying 'not in my back yard' will not achieve your aim. You need to put forward positive alternatives. This is exactly what fellow campaigner Campbell Dunford and I intended to do when we created the Renewable Energy Foundation (REF).

The twin challenges of climate change and finding enough energy to supply our country's needs might seem too large a task to be addressed by us, the public. However, when all is said and done, it is our responsibility. So, when we created REF in 2004, its remit was to conduct unbiased, factual research into renewable energy policy in the UK.

At the moment almost all attention is focused on onshore wind turbines. These are being touted as the ultimate cure for all our energy ills. However, we feel that some of the more spurious and unjustifiable claims being made about them might easily be translated into decisions that could blight the lives of many thousands of people and ruin cherished landscapes. Our aim at REF is to correct and counterbalance any inaccurate claims that we feel are being made for wind turbines. We're also looking into seeking out and developing renewable and sustainable technologies that make a difference and are realistically within our grasp

All of us have the ability and, indeed, the right to oppose inappropriate government or institutional decisions. But it must be done in a positive way. Simply pointing out errors is neither welcome nor constructive. If you truly want to change things, you have to offer alternatives.

DON'T SHARE ALL YOUR PROBLEMS ALL THE TIME

These days the workplace offers a buffet of counselling programmes, motivational workshops and courses on emotional intelligence, so it may seem ridiculous to advocate that you should leave your domestic issues outside work. But I believe you should. If someone is paying you to do a job, you should do it to the best of your ability. Obviously, a caring manager will show compassion when you experience major events such as bereavement or chronic ill-health, but I think it's important to draw a line between events that are serious life moments and things that happen to people every day. That includes relationship issues, which I firmly believe should be left at home. You're not the first person with such problems and you won't be the last. In cases like that, a problem shared is not necessarily a problem halved. If everyone started bringing their bag of woes to work with them, the atmosphere would get very miserable indeed. My point is that the work environment is not your space to treat as you wish. It's a shared space and therefore you need to think of the greater good. Either you're in reasonable shape and can come to work and make a go of it, or you're not and you can't.

That philosophy got me through a particularly challenging period in my life and ensured that I didn't 'drop the ball'. The final stage of my first marriage occurred when I was presenting *Multi-Coloured Swap Shop*. The division of assets was the relatively easy bit. The real struggle was to go into the TV studio and sparkle. But the fact that the studio was a problem-free zone helped me to pick myself up. Presenting live television for three hours requires you to maintain a high level of concentration. There is definitely no room for a hangover, irritation at the commissionaire for not letting you use the main car park, or space for painful thoughts over putting the marital home up for sale. Without this focus and determination to fence off my problems, I would probably have fallen through the floor and quite possibly destroyed my career, which was really taking off at the time. I was able to take pride in the fact that I could put my troubles to one side and give my best in the studio.

SHOW GRATITUDE TO THE PEOPLE YOU LOVE

I've gone though a very testing time in my personal life over the last couple of years, but I now know that I have a group of friends who made me feel so welcome and secure and who would literally do anything for me. For example, I was given duplicate house keys and told I could stay for as long as I wanted. My friends were in constant contact and often called simply to show their support, which was tremendous. I'm also grateful that the bond between myself and my four beautiful daughters is now stronger than ever. Never a day goes by without us talking and discussing new opportunities. Every conversation, whether face-to-face or over the telephone, ends with us saying how much we love each other. There's nothing saccharine or sticky sweet about it. We are simply displaying our genuine feelings for one another.

However positive we are about life itself, the reality is that we never know when this particular part of the journey is over. Fortunately, I frequently told my parents just how much I loved them and how grateful I was to them for everything they did for me. Even though my mother died very suddenly in 2003, I am completely at peace with the fact that I told her on many occasions just how much she meant to me. I am well aware that many people have a loved one taken from them suddenly – before they can truly express their gratitude and appreciation – which is all the more reason to make sure you do it whenever you can. Don't take anything for granted.

- ★ As part of your new positively happy regime, I want you to make sure you tell every single person you care about exactly what they mean to you. Tell them as often as possible, and even at the most unlikely times. If you can't tell them in person, call them and let them know. Do it now. Never put it off.
- ★ Don't wait for birthdays or calendar occasions to give gifts. Kindness to friends shouldn't be dictated by dates on a calendar. Go ahead and send gifts to your friends just because you want to. It doesn't have to be something expensive. The value of a gift is very often in its personalisation. It can be silly or whimsical. Even better, why not sit down and write a letter. A proper hand-written letter. I guarantee they'll never forget it.
- ★ Finally, write out everything you have to be grateful for: your health, your children, your parents, your job, your great laugh... whatever. Put it next to your bed and read it before you tuck yourself in every night.

If you approach life like this, it gets harder to be negative. And that's the plan.

A STRANGER MAY BE A FRIEND IN WAITING

We're brought up to fear people. I realise that, more than ever these days, there is a fine line between caution and paranoia and we often get the two seriously confused. I don't believe the argument that every person on the train, bus, plane or walking along the street is a threat to your security. If you buy that then you'll buy anything.

If you raise your children to adopt that attitude then don't be surprised if they are nervous. Kids don't need to be told how frightening the world can be. What they need are strategies for developing their self-esteem and self-confidence so that they can make judgements about the people they meet. You won't do them any favours by isolating them, or stopping them talking to people. Moreover, kids need to be equipped with positive messages so they can approach their lives in a confident manner.

Whether it's fear of something terrible happening, or an inherent shyness, we often avoid making eye contact in this country. We're just not good at it. The continental Europeans are, on the whole, much better at this sort of thing. They are happy to smile at the cute baby, acknowledge the elegant woman and laugh when they see something funny happen around them. We Brits, on the other hand, spend our time trying not to laugh. You know the sort of thing: the guy in the railway carriage is reading a funny book and he's laughing out loud. People get cross about it. They purse their lips and look away. They don't want to acknowledge his emotions, possibly because they're afraid of their own.

Many of us hold back because we don't feel comfortable making conversation with other people. This can be the first step in making new friends but, like most things in life, it's a lot easier if you practise.

There are a few things you can do that may help:

- ★ **Develop the habit of starting lots of small, simple conversations with a lot more people.**
- ★ **Look for areas of mutual interest. For example, if your neighbour has a beautiful garden and you're developing yours, why not ask him/her for some advice? Asking people questions can seem quite flattering to them, and they will be only too happy to respond when they see you admire their knowledge.**
- ★ **Don't expect to make witty repartee, at least not when you start. Very few people know instinctively the right things to say. The rest of us just wing it. Take your cue from the other person – and listen to him or her.**
- ★ **If you find conversation hard, then just practise acknowledging others. Don't be afraid to smile when the little boy on the bus asks funny questions of his mother and she looks round.**

It's a moment of human connection. A perfectly normal moment.

MAKE THE CONNECTION

As any psychologist will tell you, when humans do not have contact with others they soon sink into a state of despair, becoming selfish and lonely along the way. Engaging with others in a positive way – whether it's family, your community or somebody you've never met before – has immeasurable and lasting benefits for all concerned. And as far as I'm concerned, it's the difference between merely existing and really living.

Being part of the world means:

- ★ **Making a real effort to listen to others.**
- ★ **Showing our loved ones our gratitude at every opportunity.**
- ★ **Making an effort to do something positive for our communities or the world at large.**
- ★ **Remembering that others have problems too.**
- ★ **Recognising that to make new friends you will have to learn to talk to some strangers.**
- ★ **Remembering that it's not only about you – we're all in this together!**

CHAPTER 5

STAY POSITIVE IN THE FACE OF NEGATIVITY

LIKE ANYONE in the public eye, I have a relationship with the media whether I like it or not. And, as with most things in life, sometimes you like it, sometimes you don't. As I write this, I'm pretty sure that, as well as positive comments, I'm bound to get some not so favourable ones about this book. For example, one reviewer will probably come up with the 'highly amusing' alternative title of 'Positively Crappy' or perhaps 'Positively Nauseating' or (shades of Oasis here) 'Positively, Maybe?' They will not have read the book. Meanwhile, another journalist will say something along the lines of 'With this book Noel is only helping himself.' And so on.

Deep down, I know they're just doing their job. I suppose I'm fortunate in that I spent my formative career years learning my craft on radio and television in an era where there wasn't so much bandwidth to fill and journalists didn't need to seek out stories to satisfy thousands of hungry websites, newspapers and magazines, as they do today. More importantly, my wife and I had agreed that we would keep the family out of the public eye, something we found easy to do.

I won't pretend that I haven't been hurt by the media at times, and it's been hard to stomach some of the inaccurate things that have been written about me. But most of the time I just ignore it and get on with my life. I've come to the conclusion that I haven't got room to focus on unnecessary negative criticism – especially when it's not relevant to my job or doesn't come from people I respect.

If you accept the view that you're here for a good time, not a long time, you'll also accept that you need to minimise and eliminate the negatives in your life. If you fill valuable space in your brain with thoughts about people and things that annoy you, it's likely that you'll become miserable and dissatisfied at times. I'm not saying that you shouldn't give and receive constructive criticism or reflect on things that have gone wrong. But I am suggesting that you try to use the negatives as a platform from which to view your life in a more positive light. I also believe that the cosmos is less likely to be on your side if you continually focus on the negatives, and so bring yourself down. In fact, no one will want to be on your side if you adopt that position, because it means you bring them down as well.

DO YOU ENJOY ACTING HARD DONE BY?

People may feel sorry for you at first, but pretty soon they will get tired of seeing you flash your 'victim badge' and will look for ways of avoiding you. It is futile to regard yourself as a victim when there are real victims in the world – those who've suffered through war, crime and injustice, for example. Most of us have choices. They might not be the ones we want, but we have them. Despite the number of television shows urging us to write in and tell them about our dreadful holiday/builder/relationship/bank and so on, the fact is that problems are an inevitable part of life. Ultimately, the responsibility for making the best of a situation lies with you.

LIFE IS TOO SHORT TO INCLUDE NEGATIVE PEOPLE

In the previous chapter, I talked about the importance of not bringing your problems to work because of the atmosphere it creates. We spend a large part of our day in the workplace, and I think this is a very good reason to steer well clear of colleagues who whinge and moan. I make no apologies for being unequivocal about this because, aside from ruining the general atmosphere for everyone, I think negativity stifles creativity. You've probably had the experience of being in a meeting where you're tossing ideas around, just seeing what could be or might be, and someone pipes up with, 'But we can't do that because...' or, 'It won't work because...' All the creativity and spirit gets sucked out of the meeting and you're back to square one.

The result is that nothing gets off the ground or, worse still, you end up with the sort of process-led thinking that results in the compromise known as the 'five-legged camel'. I've had it happen to me and I never want to be in that situation again. Business, like life, should be inspiring, and I now refuse to work with people who continually look for problems rather than finding solutions.

The same holds true for personal relationships. No matter how much you think you love someone, if their negativity brings you down it's not a good sign. Yes, they might be cute and cuddly but if that negative side keeps coming out, it will only get worse as time goes on. If your partner is unable to understand your dreams and continually pours cold water on them, I'd suggest you change partners. Drastic? Not if you think relationships are about mutual respect and support. Think about it. What sort of future will you have with someone who can't see the positives now?

There are people who simply cannot and will not think positively, no matter what happens in their life. These people are not good for you. They won't just suffocate your ideas, they will also suffocate you. Distance yourself from them and see how high you can go.

BE CAREFUL HOW YOU CRITICISE

When I started out in radio, I accepted that I needed to learn from others and that my performances would be judged by those who were willing to employ me. As there is no definitive radio performance – no perfect wave, no killer forehand, no fastest lap – you need to work, watch others, listen to them and take their views on board.

I've always been blessed with brilliant producers and I'd like to think that, more often than not, I've heeded their advice and benefited from their suggestions. In the right professional environment, criticism is both necessary and can help improve your performance. As appraisals now play such a large part in the workplace, it's likely that at some point you will be called upon to *give* criticism, as well as receive it. In my business dealings, I've found that you get far more out of people by not taking an adversarial approach to the process. You are not there to sit in judgement on them. You're supposed to be coaching and mentoring them so that they can improve their performance.

Whether you look after a small team of people or an entire corporate army, I've found it helpful to take the following approach:

★ **Be considerate. Start by asking the person how things are going so you can get an idea of their emotional state. That will tell you whether your** tone can be crisp and brief or needs to be a little more gentle and understanding.

★ Be prompt. Criticism is not meant to be punishment. If someone hasn't been doing well, don't wait months to tell them and then use it as a stick with which to beat them. It's not fair on them or your business.

★ Be relevant. Give people specific instances of when you felt things weren't working. Don't just hit them with a blanket condemnation.

★ Look forward. Looking back is the most negative thing you can do. Constructive criticism is about the things the person can do to improve in the future.

★ Offer praise, too. Make sure you use the time to comment on what they've done well. Always thank them for their work so far.

The curse of 'celebrity'

'So what exactly do you do?' said an American lady I met at a neighbour's cocktail party. A brief description of my current activities followed and then she announced, 'Ah! I see, you're a celebrity!' Yep, here I am, in my fourth decade in the broadcasting industry and apparently now I am a 'celebrity'. The trouble with 'celebrity' is that it is one of those catch-all words that means everything – and nothing.

For more than 30 years, I've seen what I do as a professional job, requiring an apprenticeship and a lot of application and hard work. First, we were called 'broadcasters'. In the nineties we were called 'entertainers' or 'presenters'. The word 'celebrity' is one of those ambiguous terms used to describe anyone who appears on television. It also suggests success without effort, and while I'm happy for reality TV contestants to have their 15 minutes of fame, like anyone professional who has spent years learning their craft, I would like to think that 'celebrity' is more than a description that could equally well be applied to someone who streaks during a football match.

I think today's celebrity culture is a good example of how negative we've all become towards the whole concept of achievement. If achievement can be defined as exposure in a celebrity gossip magazine, how on earth are we going to cultivate real talent and enable it to rise to the surface? There is a lot of great young talent around right now. However, my concern is that, as a result of pressure to maintain a 'profile' and boost their name, these young people will not make the best choices for building their careers.

IT'S NEVER PERSONAL... WELL PERHAPS JUST A TINY BIT

You can't be successful in the broadcasting industry without the oxygen of publicity, and we all know who supplies that. As much as those of us in television often have a great deal to thank the media for in terms of the boost that they can give a career, they can also be responsible for bringing down established artists. It is rare, thankfully, but it is possible. Quite often a situation will arise in which the press, sniffing the scent of vulnerability, will pounce. It can then be a case of going from 'madcap, zany, brilliant star' to 'fallen, troubled, forgotten presenter'.

I try to be philosophical and accept that people are only doing their job. But sometimes I wonder whether it is simply an opportunity to have a stab at an easy target. Over the years, a number of people have written less than flattering comments about me which have nothing to do with my work. It all seems a bit pointless, but then maybe somebody enjoys reading the articles.

That doesn't mean I don't enjoy clever satire. I think Rory Bremner's impression of me is brilliant and so do my girls. And while John Culshaw's 'Noel Edmonds' goes for the jugular, I have to concede it is very, very good.

YOU CAN'T PLEASE YOUR AUDIENCE ALL THE TIME

Having to deal with the disapproval of other people is not easy, especially when you can't understand the motivation for their behaviour. As charming as you might be, you will never be able to please everyone. Film stars know this feeling when they get overlooked for Oscars year after year. Politicians who squeeze into marginal seats by a whisker know only too well that many of their constituents will not have voted for them. We all know how it feels.

While you may not experience personal public attacks of the sort I've described, you will invariably have to deal with what other people say about you from time to time, whether it's a former lover, colleagues, your boss, or the in-laws that never liked you in the first place. However much you try to be likeable, there will be times when you will get on the wrong side of somebody, or the chemistry will just be plain wrong. It may be because of an actual event, such as a relationship break-up, or an argument that the other party can never forget (sometimes for the rest of their lives), so feeling constantly aggrieved in your presence.

On the other hand, people will also criticise you for all sorts of irrational reasons – or simply because you're there. Your boyfriend's mates may feel threatened because you've come along on what was supposed to be a lads' night out. Your in-laws might be over-protective of their daughter. Your colleagues might think you're going to put them all out of work with your industrious ways. My advice is to learn not to let it get to you. Age and experience certainly help you deal with it but, in the meantime, if you accept that you can't change their opinion of you, the only thing you can do is build up your resistance to them.

I recommend being polite and not falling into the trap of fighting fire with fire by trying to match their negativity with your own. That tactic never works. If you get the opportunity, try to find some common ground. If they don't want to come that far, then you just have to tell yourself that you are okay. If you've done nothing to upset them, then you've nothing to feel bad about. They're the ones with the problem. Just get on and live your life and remember that there are lots of people who know you and like you and so take comfort from that.

That's what I try to do with the media. Unless, of course, they cross the line. Retaliatory action – whether it's a sarcastic comment or refusing to talk to that person – should not be at the top of your agenda. It's only an option when conciliatory action has failed. If you take the position that you have to respond to everything a colleague or a relative says, you don't leave yourself any room to move. Keep it up and you'll end up straining at the leash all the time, looking for a scrap – rather like a little dog that has absolutely no idea why he's barking at the other dogs.

RESIST THE TEMPTATION TO JOIN THE CROWD

I sometimes think we can all be overly critical of others without considering what we would do in a similar position. As a football fan, I know what it's like to give advice. Sitting in the stands, watching my team, West Ham, during the 2006 FA cup final against Liverpool, I, like many others, gave them the benefit of my point of view. Not surprisingly, they didn't take it. But with sport we all know that criticism – both useful and useless – is all part of the game and, in the majority of cases, just good-natured fun.

However, I'm not sure the same can be said of gossiping about somebody at work, especially if it becomes a regular occurrence at the coffee machine. My concern here – and many of us have done it – is that what starts off as a remark between two people soon grows into a bigger discussion in which everyone takes part, except the person concerned. For me, work is a place to be professional and to do the job you're being paid for. If gossip is personal it should be left out of the office.

If you have a professional issue to take up with somebody, then do it on a one-to-one basis and make sure your comments are constructive. This isn't just for the other person's benefit, either – it's also for your own sake. Even though you may think that you're just joining in with what everyone else is saying, you might find you're the one who is singled out as the ringleader. That's a danger of joining in with the group. What's more, if you do it often enough, they may start on you next! Perhaps it's karma, but I've seen it often enough to know that it really does work like that.

At this point, I want you to think about this: are you someone who takes every opportunity to criticise? Please understand that I'm not talking about the odd well-aimed barb or witty remark. I'm referring to setting yourself up as an arbiter of what should and shouldn't *be* – and doing so continuously.

If you *are* like this, then the only way is down. You cannot hope to be positively happy if you expend your energy in such a negative way. 'But it's just a bit of harmless fun,' you may say. Harmless fun is squirting someone with a water pistol. Character assassination, whether it's aimed at people you know or those whom you don't, is definitely not harmless. And I can think of things that are a lot more fun than cutting a person's reputation to ribbons.

A friend of mine, who is in her forties, reflects that one of her ambitions on reaching this particular stage in her life was to develop what she called 'grace'. I asked her what she meant by that and she said, 'I want to get to the point where, if I meet someone at a party who I consider to be stupid or idiotic, I no longer feel the need to put them in their place. I would like to think that I can just smile and extricate myself from the situation. I want to stop taking people on.'

Now, she's quite a sharp, vitriolic person as a rule so, as you can imagine, the temptation to display her verbal skills is always there. I asked her if she'd achieved it. 'I'm getting there,' she replied. 'I feel calmer when I do manage it.'

You become what you practise, and if you practise being spiteful, even to people who don't know you're doing it, you will become a more negative person yourself.

Beware the evil banana...

At the time of writing, bananas have not received a bad press – so far as I am aware. However, as we all know, it's rare for a day to go by without the media regaling us with the latest perils awaiting us in our daily lives. Forget the next *big* thing; instead we have the next *bad* thing, and so it's easy to feel that it won't be long before the sweet, friendly banana is demonised too – perhaps for its overly rich potassium content.

While I understand the need to raise public awareness about important issues – and I am grateful to the eminent doctors, scientists, nutritionists and others who warn us – I think it's important to keep things in perspective. This is especially so if you're the sort of person whose world is easily rocked by the latest revelations about peanuts, rogue plastic toys, killer centipedes or whatever.

Please don't think I am trivialising your fears. I'm not. I also understand that some of us are able to shrug off such things more easily then others. However, what I am asking you to do – for your own sake – is to stop, think and take a deep breath before you absorb every dire warning that is issued. Most of the time, the danger is less that something sinister will happen to you, and more that you will overload your brain with worry about what hasn't happened. This sort of thinking can send you into a negative spiral and limit your capacity for enjoyment.

My own view is that if something is going to happen to me, it will. I just don't believe that the number of so-called 'evil people' and 'tragic events' in the world has multiplied to any great extent. At the same time, I don't have the complex facts at my disposal to make sense of all the possible risks. So I would rather concentrate my efforts on dealing with what I can control. The rest is not in my hands and I'm not prepared to sacrifice my happiness worrying about things that are much bigger than me. While I will take precautions where necessary, I won't run my life on the basis of things that have not happened.

Next time someone tells you, 'Oh my God! It's all so terrible!' I want you to stop, think and breathe. Then ask them why? And think about whether their answer really negates all the positives. The same applies to the newspapers you read and the news broadcasts you watch. Ask yourself the following:

- ★ **Are there any actual facts in this piece? (That is, verifiable facts, ones that can be backed up, not just, 'A government spokesman said…').**
- ★ **Where is the evidence for this item? (That is, hard data, not estimates or, 'The man believes he saw...').**
- ★ **Is there another side to the story? (Usually, the answer is yes!)**
- ★ **Is it rational for me to be worried about this at this stage? (Most likely not!)**
- ★ **Will it affect my life as of today? (Again, most likely not!)**

In 99.9 per cent of cases, there is really nothing that should worry you. And that other 0.1 per cent? Well, sometimes you can do something, such as launch a local campaign. But at other times there is little you can do, other than leave it in the hands of God, the cosmos or whatever. We can't control everything and if we try we will just end up making ourselves very ill, often for no reason at all. Accept that the world is going to continue to be a place full of uncertainties but that uncertainty can mean many good things as well as bad.

MAKE FRIENDS WITH YOUR LOWS

Being positively happy is about learning to manage the negative moments so that they don't have a seismic effect on your overall self-esteem and well-being. Negative thoughts have a way of migrating from your brain into your body and, as countless medical people acknowledge, can actually make you physically ill. If you are physically and emotionally fragile, then it's even more vital that you keep the negative forces at a distance because they will surely sap all your energy.

Have you noticed how just thinking about something negative – say, a bad day at work, or a row with your partner, or getting cross with your children – makes you feel tired and listless? The inability to neutralise those feelings and shake them off means that they'll just hang around, manifesting themselves in disorders such as migraines, backache, digestive problems or whatever, depending on where you are physically weakest.

The people who cope best with negative feelings are

those who recognise them as a necessary and relevant part of their personal growth, rather than as an aberration. Instead of wasting energy resisting their lows, they make friends with them. Positively happy people accept that feelings such as these come and go in cycles. They tell themselves that the bad times are a normal part of life and will eventually move on. You often see this acceptance in people who have fought their way back from a really tough period in their lives. They just seem to come back with an ability to see life much more clearly.

A very good friend of mine, whom I will refer to as Jimmy, has struggled with the challenge of alcohol addiction for more than 30 years. Even though he's been 'dry' for the last 20 years, he still describes himself as an alcoholic. He recognises that even as little as a single glass of wine would change his personality dramatically and impact negatively on all those around him. Getting to the point of acknowledgement is, of course, the alcoholic's greatest challenge. Jimmy arrived there only after hitting what he described as 'absolute rock bottom'. He now does a lot of unpaid work for those less fortunate than himself: those who are unable to acknowledge the power of their addiction.

He is also the greatest friend anyone could wish for and, having endured a long negative period in his own life, he absolutely radiates positivity to others. My capacity to face personal difficulties of my own over the past few years has been greatly strengthened by Jimmy. Never a week has gone by without a phone call, however brief, enquiring about my well-being. His ability to see things with great clarity has, I think, been intensified by adversity. Nobody could ask for a more powerful friendship and I will be in his debt forever. If you're going through a particularly difficult period in your life, I urge you to find yourself a Jimmy.

If you're feeling low about a particular issue and just can't seem to shake off negative thoughts, try asking yourself how much the problem will matter in, say, three months, six months, or a year. Missed opportunities, disagreements, mistakes at work, financial difficulties, whatever the problem might be, in the general scheme of things will be as irrelevant as bumps in the road as time goes by. By recasting your thoughts in this way you can develop a more rational, less emotionally driven perspective of the situation and this can help to lift your spirits.

Another way of dealing with the anxiety generated by negative thoughts is to ask yourself, 'What's the absolute worst that can happen?' You get a lower mark than you expected in an exam. You say the wrong thing in a job interview. Is it really going to destroy your life? Of course not.

Accept that negatives are valid components of your life. If you can see that they are part of life's jigsaw puzzle, you will be able to relax and learn from them so that, gradually, they bother you less and less.

THE RIGHT KIND OF POSITIVE

While it's important to deal with negativity in a positive way, there are situations where being too positive may not be appropriate. A friend of mine was recently talking about her best friend who is desperately trying to have her second baby but has now had three consecutive miscarriages. At the time of writing her friend is pregnant again but, understandably, worried that the same thing might happen.

As my friend says, 'How much positivity can you bring to such a situation? I mean what is appropriate? You can't pretend you understand because you don't. You can't tell her it's going to be fine this time because you're not in a position to say that. On the other hand, do you just sit there and agree with her when she says she thinks it's going to go wrong?'

We've all been in these situations where we desperately want to help a friend through their moment of pain but are terrified of making it worse and appearing useless. For some people it's tempting to try and 'own' the problem even though it's not theirs to own. By that I mean that instead of maintaining some sort of distance, they get totally involved in the minutiae of what their friend is going through. This can easily lead to endless discussions that go round in circles; you realise you're not helping and they don't feel any better. I'm not saying don't talk about it but over the years my experiences with a whole range of people have led me to believe that I have to accept that, try as I might, I cannot solve their problems for them. Just like they cannot solve mine for me.

On the other hand, that doesn't mean I can't listen to them. And sometimes that's exactly what people want you to do. If you think about the times when you've felt alone with your fears – perhaps waiting for the results of a medical test – all you really want is someone to be there. Deep down you know they can't get you out of the situation but just having them around, making cups of tea for you, can provide the respite you need. And that's what you need to do for others. Simply be there. As banal and simple as it sounds, sometimes that is all your role demands. It may not sound particularly positive but to the person concerned just knowing that someone is there provides all the positivity they need.

SEE YOUR PROBLEMS AS A SIGNAL FOR CHANGE

What would happen if you were to look at your problems as a sign that something had to change? For example, do you find that, despite your best intentions, you are often misunderstood by people? While it might be easy to get annoyed with them, have you analysed the pattern and wondered if you had something to do with it? Instead of using up energy being frustrated every time the problem manifests itself, why not try to get to the bottom of it. Perhaps if you decided to spend a little more time considering what you were going to say before saying it, the problem could be averted.

Young, hopeful and far too thin-skinned

I can still vividly remember the very first time I opened a publication and saw that I was the subject of a vitriolic attack. In retrospect, it was probably extremely mild by today's journalistic standards. *Disc and Music Echo* was a pop paper that sought to rival the success of *Melody Maker* and the *NME*. The magazine is now long gone, but the gist of the attack was that I had dared to take over from Kenny Everett after he'd been sacked by the BBC. I always knew that Kenny was going to be a tough act to follow. Believe me, the guy was my hero, so the challenge was already enormous and very frightening. As I recall, the article was no more than a paragraph, but at the time it really affected me.

Of course I knew Kenny was an icon (and I can't think of anyone who could follow him today) but, as for today's radio presenters, it's a case of turning in a professional performance and making the programme your own. Show the public you have your own style and integrity and that you're not trying to replace a hero and there is a good chance they will eventually warm to you. (It actually took me nine months to rebuild the audience figures and no doubt there are radio fanatics who have still to accept me – but that's just the way it is and I'm fine with that.)

I think I must have a streak of masochism in me because I cut out the article and dwelt on every single word. I've probably still got it somewhere in one of the scrap books that my late mother kept. The comments in those few brief sentences were hardly constructive. It was basically: 'Kenny is a radio genius and you are not worthy to fill his time slot.' I couldn't have agreed more. I knew I wasn't in his league and therefore I didn't try to fill his shoes. I just tried to do the best I could do.

The article really knocked my confidence. You need a lot of self-belief to go into a studio and talk into the air, believing that you have the attention of the listener or viewer. I just had to pick myself up and keep going.

Negativity is not bad in itself; it's how you choose to react to it that matters. For example:

- ★ **Look at yourself before judging others.**
- ★ **Don't think of yourself as a victim.**
- ★ **Distance yourself from negative people.**
- ★ **Don't pick on others to make yourself feel better.**
- ★ **Don't allow the scaremongers to influence your thoughts.**
- ★ **Be thoughtful in the way you deliver criticism.**
- ★ **Accept that people don't always move in rational ways.**

CHAPTER 6

LEARN TO WELCOME CHANGE

WE SPEND MUCH of our lives seeking security, so it's no surprise that many of us find the idea of change quite scary. Fundamentally, we're creatures of habit, so very often the impetus for change only comes when something quite significant happens to force it upon us. For the most part we're happy to stay in the comfort of what we know while a whole world of opportunities remains waiting to be explored.

While there are difficult life changes that we all have to go through, change is not always negative. It can also be a chance to discover new dimensions to our character and free ourselves from self-imposed limitations. If we are brave enough to allow even a small amount of uncertainty into our lives, we have more chance of discovering new avenues of satisfaction and happiness.

Of course, it won't be easy. At times it will even be frightening, but then so is the idea of living your life doing the same things all the time, never knowing what it's like to take even the smallest step into the unknown. As they say, you have to speculate to accumulate.

WHEN CHANGE CHOOSES YOU

For over two decades, I pretty much knew what I was supposed to be doing. While I worked on different radio and television shows, I had an established 'home' at the BBC and things were pretty predictable and secure. After I left the BBC at the end of my five-year contract, I received numerous offers to return to radio or television. None compared with my previous experiences and, with dramatic changes to the industry taking place, I was frankly quite happy to be out of it.

Legions of makeover shows paved the way for reality television of the type that didn't appeal to me and, to this day, still doesn't. When I look at the schedules over the last five or six years, it's difficult to see where Noel Edmonds would have fitted in anyway. Every format has its time and *Noel's House Party* had definitely run its course. Whenever I'm asked whether I want to bring it back, my reply is that it's already been made over and re-launched. It's now called *Ant and Dec's Saturday Takeaway* and they do a bloody good job, too.

I won't deny that I felt very lost and wasn't sure what I was supposed to be doing. That piece of self-knowledge also prevented me from rushing into anything else. Fortunately, my financial position was such that I could afford to step away from broadcasting. But, if I'm honest, I didn't feel that secure about anything. I'd spent a long time in one place, and while it was time to sample some other delights, that possibility was both exciting and scary. One of the things I had to adapt to was the way Noel Edmonds was now seen by the media and the public. It really didn't bother me to be occasionally described as an 'ex-TV presenter' or 'former *House Party* star'. The only time it rankled was when the press tried to paint a picture of a broken, lonely man polishing his trophies and praying that the phone would ring. I suppose having been cheery Noel for so long, I didn't want people to think that I wasn't.

I soon got used to my new life and learned to embrace it and the positives that came with it. For example, as the recognition factor diminished, simple everyday tasks such as shopping with the family became more pleasant. (I'll be honest, though, the best table in the restaurant wasn't always forthcoming, and the automatic airline upgrades quickly ceased! But that's the way it goes.) Life in Devon was sweet and, best of all, for the first time in my life I found out what it was like to be a proper father. But, with the arrival of my fourth daughter, I was now able to dedicate even more time to this wonderful little person. I've never shied away from my fatherly duties but it was a joy to be there for most of my daughter's bath times. Had I continued my BBC life, all of these wonderful pleasures would have been denied to me and, indeed, to her.

The further I got away from the memory of my BBC career, the happier I became. While I didn't know it then, it was time for a change. What happened had happened for a reason. Perhaps the cosmos figured that I'd taken too long to make the decision myself, so it was made for me. Maybe it was time for me to slow down. Perhaps it was time for me to spend more time in the real world and less in TV land.

When you find yourself in a situation in which you haven't chosen change and it has been chosen for you, don't focus on the negatives. Recognise your fears but try to see the positives.

LET GO OF YOUR LIMITATIONS

Are you the sort of person who won't invite people to dinner because you can't cook? Or won't go running in the park because you think you'll look silly? Or perhaps you won't apply for a particular job because you know you won't get it.

All of these are self-imposed limitations. They're thoughts that you've had so often that you've made them real. You need to apply some truthful thinking to them. For example, perhaps you can't cook a Michelin-standard meal, but there is bound to be something simple that you can cook. Similarly, you might want to go running in the park but are worried about how you look. Just remember that other people are too busy thinking of other things to look at you. Alternatively, while you might not fit the exact job specification on paper, you just never know whether you and the interviewer will hit it off, thus improving your chances of getting the job.

If you have spent most of your life defining your limitations and telling yourself that you can't change careers because you have a mortgage or you can't move abroad because you'll miss your parents, then you need to rewrite the script so that your brain gets used to the idea that you can. Many of our limitations come from our upbringing and are reinforced by friends and family, so they can be pretty tough to leave behind.

We spend years fine-tuning these limitations, which can encompass everything from the foods we won't eat to the countries we would never go to (even though we know nothing about them) or the hair colour of our potential partners. Changing our behaviour means undoing those years of conditioning and altering our views about what we can do.

It also means not thinking too much about the action you're about to undertake. I know someone who had trouble learning to dive from the side of a pool. The reason why she had problems was that, instead of just following her instincts, she over-analysed the whole thing. And the more she thought about it, the more she believed she couldn't do it. She spent most of the time at the edge of the pool looking in.

The psychologists call this behaviour paralysis by analysis. It describes the tendency to question every single aspect of a potential action to the point where we talk ourselves out of it. People who are like this are often looking for guarantees. But life doesn't come with any. If it did, then taking a risk would not be a risk. It wouldn't be exciting. We wouldn't anticipate things as much as we do or get that adrenaline rush that many of us crave. Fear is a natural reaction, in that it is supposed to make us stop and think before we do something. The problem is when our self-imposed limitations dictate our actions and hold us back.

A very good way to prepare for major changes is to start by making some relatively minor ones. Change your breakfast. Change your route to work. Change your hair and your clothes. Try a new flavour of tea. Order something in a restaurant that you always wanted to try but kept telling yourself you might not like. Become accustomed to the idea of a life where change is part of the norm. Why not try to do one thing differently each day?

This is also the time to practise your self-focus and to visualise the change you want to make so that your brain can buy in to the idea. If you do your homework and visualise yourself as successfully making the move then it's likely that you will fulfil your desire.

If you really want to do something but you're constantly asking yourself, 'What happens if I do?' turn the question round and ask yourself, 'What happens if I don't?'

In a sense, that's what I had to ask myself when I was offered *DoND*. I was apprehensive at first. Honestly! I really was so unsure about it. I'd spent several years away from television and had got used to my new life. I wasn't short of things to do and was quite busy with my businesses. And I didn't need the money. At the same time, I was very uncertain about how I'd be received by the public. I've said elsewhere in the book that I knew the show would be a success, regardless of who hosted it, because it was that sort of format. Was I ready to return to the public eye and put myself back on the line?

Anyway, after a great deal of discussion with family and assorted trusted people, I went ahead and did it. That first day I walked into the studio I was, to put it mildly, very apprehensive. I was surrounded by new faces. New *very young* faces. The youngest members of the team were probably at school when I was last on television. Some of the production team probably wondered what I'd be like to work with and all were no doubt wondering if the show would be a success. Add to the mix 22 nervous contestants and an inquisitive audience and you actually have all the ingredients for a disaster. So I just followed my own principles of self-focus and got on with it. These days that initial discomfort has turned to positive comfort.

DEAL OR NO DEAL – MONEY IS NOT THE ONLY REWARD

For the contestants on *DoND*, the show is a major step out of their comfort zone. It's fair to assume that people want to be on the show primarily to win money and that's what we want them to do as well. To get to that point, however, they often go through a set of experiences that result in the money becoming irrelevant. The effects frequently continue long after we have bidden the contestants farewell, and it has nothing to do with being on television.

Now I'm well aware that the phrases 'life-changing' and 'light entertainment' don't generally belong together but such experiences really can happen on a show like *DoND*. I think some of the contestants' stories are interesting in that they show how new experiences can reward us in ways we don't expect.

Lucy Harrington was one of those people. Lucy holds the distinction of being with us for a record 50 shows – and winning a fiver. She describes herself as a risk-taker (when she was 18 she took her gap year in Brazil) and someone who doesn't normally think too much about things. 'I watched the show on TV one day and thought, "Anyone can do that. You don't have to be clever." And I was pretty broke.' Having spent so long in the company of both contestants and production crew before she went on, Lucy had become part of the furniture.

By the time her turn came, she wasn't really thinking about the money, 'I just didn't want to go home. I was having such a good time meeting people I would never normally associate with in my daily life and had become much more confident than when I arrived.' Perhaps it was the surprise of finally getting into the hot seat, but when Lucy's turn finally came she says she acted completely out of character – and ended up with just £5.

'I wasn't bothered. I was more bothered about having to go home and back to my old life. It actually took me a few weeks to think about the money and when I did it only stayed in my head for about two days. I definitely learned that money is not my overriding priority. You know, I hadn't ever thought about spending the money, like some people do. Not everyone can be a winner. What I got was what I was supposed to get out of it.

'I was lucky because I had that chance to find myself. When I got home, all my friends said that I was happier and I'd changed. One even said I had a sparkle in my eyes. Oh, and I also learned to wear makeup for the first time in my life. Now I wear it all the time.'

As Nick Bain puts it, 'You see a normal guy win a huge amount of money so you don't think of anything less than success.' Nick won just 1p and, like Lucy, has my admiration for the way he handled himself in the circumstances. 'Initially, I had to get used to being away from my wife and son for two and half weeks, which was a new experience. I'd watched others take risks and that only made me feel more confident. I'd always joked about winning 1p but never believed it would happen.' Nick was hugely devastated at the end of his game and everyone felt for him. 'The fact that I'd blown my big chance was bad enough. On top of that, all the other contestants were crying. Then I had to tell my wife, so it was pretty heavy. She thought I was joking!

'After that, I just accepted it. Sure it played on my brain for two or three days and the money would have come in handy, but my life is no different from the way it was before. I didn't lose anything. I'm still here. I'm still Nick, and I made loads of new friends.'

While Morris Simpson liked the idea of winning a lot of money, his prime ambition was much more about creating a big moment. 'I wanted to be known as the first winner of £250,000. I really wanted that honour.' He is someone with an extraordinary amount of self-belief, a naturally positive person. Watching him play, you knew he just felt he should keep going. There was absolutely no hint of self-doubt. When the game got down to two boxes, Morris had £20,000 and £250,000 remaining. At this point he describes his head as 'being in a vice'. Offered £101,000 by the banker, he turned it down and opened his box to reveal £20,000. Not bad, but he could have had five times more.

Of course, I wanted him to take the banker's offer, but as with all contestants, I have to keep my emotions hidden. You just know how much the money would help. But I think Morris's sense of destiny drove him on. He really believed he was going to be the first. 'I wanted to finish the game,' he says. Morris's personality caught the eye of an events entrepreneur who was watching the show. As a consequence, Morris has taken on the role of master of ceremonies and, with his sunny nature, I'm sure he'll go on to good things.

As the experiences of these contestants show, you can't always get what you want but you can often get something else that is just as rewarding. All these people demonstrate that, even if the action you take doesn't enable you to achieve your original aim, you can still get something equally rewarding out of it and learn more about yourself. In other words, nothing is wasted.

When the dream goes horribly wrong

I had piloted helicopters for more than 25 years without any serious incident and had long held the dream of owning a twin-engine helicopter. The challenge of flying a craft that was quicker and apparently safer than my faithful single-engine machine excited me, rather as learning to fly had done all those years ago. The reason that I took up flying in the first place was to give myself a challenge, and this was just an extension of that. Six years ago I passed the exams I needed to take to fly this particular helicopter. I set off to Italy to collect my new aircraft and fly it back to my home in Devon.

Shortly after I returned, the helicopter started to develop problems. I wondered if I'd got a bad one! On one occasion, I took off from the London heliport and as I climbed over the roof top of Buckingham Palace, all hell broke loose in the cockpit and an alarm sounded warning me that I'd lost oil pressure. On another occasion, I apparently had a major engine fire and, from then on, there seemed to be an endless stream of things going wrong.

There was worse to come. One day, flying from Devon to London, the helicopter's stabilisation system developed a serious fault. I only realised this when, at 1,000 feet south of Taunton, the helicopter suddenly attempted to fly upside down! It was as if a giant hand had come out of the sky and grabbed the rear of the helicopter. Fortunately, with just a few hundred feet to go, I was able to regain control of the aircraft. But I can tell you that I didn't stop shaking for days. The incident shook my confidence as a pilot and I haven't taken the controls of a helicopter since that day. I don't mind being piloted by others and I still regularly use helicopters. But not that type.

Even after I'd sent the aircraft back to the manufacturers, the emotional ramifications continued. It was hard to take something positive out of the experience. Eventually I managed to tell myself that had my family been on board or had I chosen to climb into cloud as I was tempted to do, things could have been worse. I'd had 25 years of piloting helicopters so maybe it was time to move on to something else.

COPING WITH THE STRESS OF CHANGE

Coping with a new marriage, new home, new baby, new job, a divorce or the death of a loved one are some of the most challenging changes one can face. Everyone knows that such levels of change can be very stressful and difficult to cope with. But small changes can have a big impact too, though this is often underestimated.

Change is stressful because it requires us to adjust our lives and to alter established patterns of behaviour that we've followed for a long time. For example, when you break up with someone you've been with for many years, you don't just say goodbye to that person but also to a whole lifetime of routines and patterns that you've got used to. If you've been made redundant from your job, you'll know it's not just about losing a pay packet and the subsequent hardship, it's also about losing contact with the people you've worked with and with the sense of camaraderie, about no longer having a place to go where, as they used to say in the TV series *Cheers*, 'Everybody knows your name.'

When the world you've created with someone is falling down around you, I believe it's important to concentrate on what you can salvage from it – and I don't mean material things – rather than the things you can do nothing about. If you've decided that a relationship is dead and buried, then there is no point raking it over. The fact of the matter is that, unless you've only been married for a few months, the relationship will have been falling apart for some time. You will already have expended a great deal of time and effort in trying to keep it together and, if you have now reached the stage where you have decided that the only solution is to split up, you have already been through a great deal. Most people don't take such decisions lightly or quickly.

When my second marriage failed, my major concern was to look after my daughters and make sure that they were coping. So I focused my energies on them. By doing that, I think the process was far less destructive for everybody than it would otherwise have been. I'm not going to pretend it was easy but, as I've said elsewhere in the book, I had friends who looked after me and gave me a great deal of support. And frankly, I think when you're in the middle of something like that, that's the most you should expect from yourself. It's totally unrealistic to expect to feel better immediately when you've gone through a major life change. In fact, I think contriving to convince yourself that you are suddenly feeling better is actually bad for you. Accepting that you need time just to be and take it all in is, I believe, very important.

These days, even though my second marriage is over, my own and my ex-wife's joint responsibility as parents most certainly is not, and we are determined to ensure that our girls have the love, security and opportunities they need. The happy place in which I find myself with my daughters these days is undoubtedly down to our ability as a group of individuals to turn negative thoughts into positive actions. I am really proud that we have emerged from bitter disappointment and deep sadness to reach a position of stability and happiness. It's wonderful to hear the girls now talk with such enthusiasm about the years at Broomford (our former family house in Devon) and they have a genuine gratitude for everything that their parents achieved for them.

In 2006, my three eldest daughters chose to accompany me to the BAFTA awards ceremony. When I walked down the red carpet with these three elegant young ladies, I nearly choked with pride and happiness.

TAKE A DIFFERENT POINT OF VIEW

Being creatures of habit, we tend to look for ways to reinforce our thoughts and actions. That means we read and listen to opinions that we know will match our own general view of life and don't really give much time to anyone who doesn't. Taking such an inflexible position means we're closing ourselves off from learning something new. I'm not saying you need to change your views but I am suggesting that it's good to look at things from a different perspective. You will invariably learn something new. And you will condition yourself not to be so stubborn and resistant to new ideas. You'll also be better prepared to cope with the idea of change.

I'll admit that the past six years have been a major exercise in change for me. I won't say I'm great at stepping out of my comfort zone but I reckon I'm getting there and I have a sense that the cosmos is willing me to go onwards and upwards. What that means right now, I don't really know. However, I do know that, as a result of having had changes imposed on my life, I am now less afraid of seeking them out myself and I do believe the best years of my life are yet to come.

Anything we haven't thought or done – anything new – lies outside the parameters of our comfort zone. When we start thinking or doing these things, we often feel uncomfortable. And, after feeling uncomfortable, we sometimes get discouraged and tend to give up before ever starting something new. Certainly, the changes I've experienced over the past few years have opened my eyes to all sorts of new possibilities I would not have contemplated before.

Change shouldn't only be something you wait for but also something you seek:

- ★ **Don't see change as inherently bad.**
- ★ **Don't live by self-imposed limitations.**
- ★ **Prepare for major changes by making smaller ones.**
- ★ **Seek out views that are different from your own.**
- ★ **When change is difficult, focus only on what you can control.**
- ★ **Recognise that as one door closes another opens.**

CHAPTER 7

BE A POSITIVE PARENT

MY PARENTS gave three fundamental gifts to their only son – love, security and opportunity. They believed that these ingredients would enable me to cope with whatever life dished up. I appreciated everything they did for me at the time, but I suppose it is only since they passed away that I have truly understood their legacy.

I also know how difficult it is to try to do something you feel should be completely natural and instinctive and yet which can become incredibly complicated. In my case, the challenges of a career in the spotlight, together with divorce, have certainly tested my ability to remain a consistently positive parent.

Although my professional life involves a medium that delivers fantasies, I don't believe it's possible to play jolly happy families all the time. I do believe, however, that by taking a positive approach to parenthood, by providing discipline, guidance and love, and instilling responsibility, our children will be able to take on the world – with or without us.

CHILDREN ARE NOT COMPLICATED

I have a problem with the fact that the word 'parent' has turned into 'parenting'. This 'parenting' is everywhere. There are endless magazines devoted to it. We humans have only survived thus far because we know how to raise children. Our parents did well enough without 'parenting' advice. They didn't have to contend with opinions in magazines – and with other parents trying to make them feel guilty as a consequence of these opinions – and they didn't over-analyse the task.

Today (and I'll admit this is a problem mainly seen in affluent, middle-class families) there is an entire industry around parenthood. Parents are encouraged to enrol their children in a different activity every night after school. Instead of letting them enjoy their childhood, they bundle them off to classes in toddler calculus or something equally ridiculous. You almost get the impression that unless little Rupert has an MBA by the age of 10 or little Persephone is in the Bolshoi by the time she's eight, their parents' efforts will be in vain.

Instead of using common sense, many of us fall into the trap of listening to the reams of advice that seems to be growing daily. I'm not talking about the core of good books that are out there (authors like Steve Biddulph and that guru of tough love Dr Phil McGraw talk a lot of sense) but there's a great deal of psychobabble about childhood behaviour. Instead of tuning in to their children, many parents seem intent on putting their own spin on their child's actions. You know the way it works: a child behaves in a way that's a bit different or unusual, and the parents over-analyse it and fear the worst.

Children are so much fun to be around because their behaviour is simple and free of artifice. They don't disguise their feelings, and they don't really think about why they do things. Remember that next time you are shocked or surprised by something your toddler does. They do things mostly because they've just discovered they can. Therefore we should respond to them in the way in which they reveal themselves – simply and without complication. Children aren't there to be processed, they're there to be nurtured and loved and given the freedom to live their own lives.

DON'T FEEL GUILTY FOR WHAT YOU CAN'T BE

I often hear people commenting on how to be a good parent. I'm not sure what it really means, however. As a dad myself, there are times I feel guilty because I can't answer a simple question, such as, 'Where exactly is Timbuktu?' Many new parents put themselves through hell trying to be perfect – doing everything and being all things to their children. But really it doesn't have to be so complicated.

Life pushes us all to the limit. If you don't find it difficult to be a parent sometimes, then you're not human. But I'm grateful my parents encouraged me to adopt their mantra of love, security and opportunity. And isn't that really what being a good parent is all about? If you ensure your children have those three things, then you've done a pretty good job, in my opinion. Give your children all the love and security you can to help guide them to opportunity. They will see it and know it and love you for it.

IT HELPS IF THEY SEE YOU ARE HAPPY

In the late nineties, I led an extremely hectic life. In addition to *Noel's House Party*, my company, Unique Group, had a commercial arrangement with the BBC that allowed us to exploit the intellectual property rights of the show. We licensed theme parks, merchandise and spin-off events. Mr Blobby became a phenomenon that exists to this day (even though he's taking a sabbatical). I made a documentary series about my two-car entry in the 1997 Le Mans 24-hour race. The BBC asked me to launch the National Lottery TV programme and I formed new companies dealing with videoconferencing and business consultancy as well as radio, TV and video production.

It was an extraordinarily exciting time and I threw myself into my work with great energy and commitment. During my final five years with the BBC, I was doing almost 50 shows a year. That might not seem much when compared with the 300 a year I'm doing now with *Deal or No Deal*. But *House Party* had a voracious appetite for creative material and although the public only saw it on air each Saturday for half of the year, the rest of the time was spent feeding the monster.

I was also doing nearly 30 shows a year from the BBC's Pebble Mill studios, in Birmingham: *Telly Addicts*, the spin-offs *Noel's Addicts* and *Noel's Telly Years*. Each Christmas I would add to this workload by undertaking a gruelling four-week filming schedule for my annual Christmas show, *Noel's Christmas Presents*. We were also farming 850 acres of exquisite Devon countryside.

During press interviews, I was continually being asked whether I was a workaholic. At the time I always denied the charge, but in retrospect perhaps I did do a little too much. In terms of family life, while I wasn't around for day-to-day duties and dare not claim I made visits to the supermarket (as film and television people seem to want to do these days) our time together as a family was good.

Even though my recording schedule was punishing at times and took me away from home for many days at a time, I would always try as hard as I could to get back to my wife and children. It mattered a lot to me to grab even the shortest period of time with my family. Of course, I did have an enormous advantage over most working fathers in that the girls could see the fruits of my labours on the television screen. They have always been incredibly loyal viewers of my shows and visited the studios whenever they could. I never felt they did this out of duty – in fact, quite the opposite.

No, they didn't have me all the time but, speaking to them about it recently, they recalled that when I did arrive home I would bring with me a lot of stories about my adventures. They would sit around until I'd bored them stupid (not always) with anecdotes. They particularly remember the ones from *Noel's Christmas Presents.*

So we had our family moments, and I'd like to think that what they didn't get in quantity I made up for in quality. They knew I wasn't neglecting them for spurious reasons and that my work was important to me. It wasn't a conventional routine. I wasn't home by 6 pm every evening. But I did try to make the most of the time we had together.

The girls knew that I loved what I did and perhaps realised that their dad was fulfilled. That would have sent out a positive signal. If I had come home and whinged about my work, I think it would have been different and I might have generated much resentment. Even though there's been a big change in our family dynamics, when we do all get together we are still very much 'Team Edmonds'. I am a very lucky man.

THE GREATEST GIFT IS YOUR ATTENTION

When the girls were younger, we would have our 'God bless' ritual each evening. This was a moment of tranquillity and reflection at the end of a busy day. No matter whether they were tired from school or I was exhausted from work, we would clear our minds and say thank you as a family. There was a role call of family and friends (including those 'in heaven') and then individual thank yous for the events of the day. Sometimes it would finish with a discussion. Nothing heavy, just a family appreciation for what we had all experienced and, of course, what we were looking forward to in the future. We tried to do it every day without fail.

Even if you can't be with your children all the time, the greatest gifts you can give them when you are there are your time and attention. From that they will gain acceptance, self-respect, encouragement and security. In turn, they will learn to respect other people – their teachers, for example. Children who know they are being listened to will feel loved, respected and secure. They will know their opinions are worth listening to and so will feel more comfortable about telling you things. Thus you begin a cycle that is extremely positive. They will also feel more comfortable about speaking up outside the home. I really think this is something people must understand – rather than blaming children for not listening.

FIND YOUR OWN WORK-LIFE BALANCE

Maybe my balance between work and family wasn't textbook, but it seemed to work for our family. Indeed, my daughters tell me that having me at home so much over the past few years has not been easy!

I appreciate that there is a lot of insecurity in the workplace today. Many people feel that unless they're actually on the premises their job is under threat. But there are no guarantees. You can give your employer every last drop of blood, sweat and tears and still get fired. If your relationship or health suffer, and you can't look after your family, what is the point? I know of someone in Australia who postponed a trip to see his ageing mother in the UK at the behest of his boss. Fate stepped in and his mother died before he could see her. Did his work thank him for it? No way. Did he regret it? I imagine it is a wound that will never heal.

As I write this, the Chartered Management Institute has brought out a survey – in time for the summer holidays – that reports, among other things, that managers collectively sacrifice around 19 million days of holiday each year. A third of these blamed their heavy workload. Others say they found it hard to let go of their responsibilities. What was most disturbing was that some managers said they would gladly negotiate shorter holidays in return for other benefits – such as money.

I can understand this attitude if you're struggling to make ends meet, but the people we're talking about are well paid. What's more, there is no such thing as an empty in-tray. If you accept that, then surely you must accept that missing the holidays you are paid to take is utterly misplaced and futile. It's a shame they didn't survey the number of managers that get ill through overwork. I'm sure it would have been high.

OPPORTUNITY WITHOUT RESPONSIBILITY IS WASTED

While my mum and dad were the most wonderful parents anybody could wish for, there was absolutely nothing to suggest that Lydia and Dudley Edmonds were actually going to produce a boy who had such ludicrous ambitions. Nobody in our family had been even vaguely associated with the entertainment industry.

However, I understand from his past pupils that my father's history lessons were spectacular and enjoyable, and as a headmaster, he could effortlessly command the stage at the annual prize giving. Dear old mum used to enjoy her moments of attention and glory, too, particularly in the later years on the golf course. She moved to Devon so she could be closer to us and became instantly popular in the local village pub. She would never miss an opportunity to point out to complete strangers who her son was. While my initial reaction was to cringe, it was fantastic to realise just how proud my parents were of their only child. Like many parents, they would probably have said they would have liked to give me more, yet what they gave me was all I needed to get going.

Now, you may say it's a different story for my own children, because I am comfortably off and so they can have anything they want. Not really. My financial status certainly doesn't mean they get any more love or security than my parents gave me or any parent can give their children. However, I am aware that they have opportunities that many other children will not have, and they are fortunate to have those options in their lives.

By opportunities I do not mean giving them everything they want or everything I am capable of giving them. Of course, they have been given some wonderful presents and have had the privilege of living in a beautiful home and riding their own horses. I won't deny that. However, I think, my ex-wife and I were always conscious that they should not be spoilt to the extent that it would affect their ability to be responsible, compassionate and productive human beings.

I have a very strong belief that opportunity needs to be given with the expectation of responsibility. If you are going to give your children something they want, then you must set parameters or goals so they know what they are expected to deliver in return. We've always brought up our children to believe that they could do anything they wanted – as long as they worked for it. When my two eldest daughters showed a real talent as equestrians it meant a huge commitment from their mother and I, in terms of time as well as money. However, we didn't go on about the sacrifices involved in taking them into international competition; I don't believe that approach motivates children to pursue something – whether it's guitar lessons, ballet or their desire to go to drama school. Our girls knew that *they* had a commitment to themselves – that they had undertaken a responsibility. I like to think that was because their mother and I always apply ourselves to new tasks with discipline and commitment. They knew that, even with their natural talent, they still had to put in the hours. And they did.

HOW MUCH CAN YOU PROTECT YOUR CHILDREN?

It's a funny old world when you can't even take your 16-year-old daughter to a discreet restaurant in a West Country city for a birthday celebration without attracting the attention of the photographers. (By 'discreet' I mean definitely not a celebrity watering hole.) The fact that wc were all together as a family enjoying a special moment led one tabloid newspaper to conclude that my ex-wife and I were getting back together again. In fact, we were doing what any family would do and giving our daughters a wonderful time on a special anniversary. If you're in a position to put aside your differences occasionally – compartmentalise them, if you like – and just think about having a good time, then it helps enormously.

I think it is reasonable to say that we managed to do a good job of raising our children. Credit for much of this was due to their mother, since I was away working. They had a wonderful lifestyle and, while we tried desperately not to spoil them, they have had some incredible experiences.

I'm particularly pleased with the way they were protected from publicity. It helped that the current crop of celebrity gossip magazines weren't around for a lot of my career; in any case it never entered our minds to expose our children to the madness of the media and we always said no to requests for photographs. This undoubtedly meant that when my three eldest daughters accompanied me to the BAFTA awards, everyone wondered who the three gorgeous ladies were with 'that bloke Edmonds'.

My three eldest daughters are now of an age when they can make their own decisions. While they took the BAFTA evening in their stride and enjoyed the novelty of a rare day out in their dad's working environment, they each value their privacy and freedom and have chosen to lead their daily lives in such a way as to protect it.

Of course, most of the time the stuff you worry about is their safety, who they associate with, their health and their happiness. I think it is important to distinguish between normal parental concerns and fretting unnecessarily. It's normal for any parent to worry about their children, but I reckon you need to be careful about letting those worries impinge on their lives to the extent that they're afraid to do anything at all. By worrying you project negative energy and it doesn't do you or your children a bit of good. In fact, when children are aware that their parents are worried about them they feel that they are not trusted, and that makes them more anxious.

Admittedly, there are times when our worries are well founded. Even then, instead of imagining the worst possible scenario, try to focus on the positive outcome that you desire and on actions that can help to bring it about. Ultimately, it's going to depend on factors such as where you live, how emotionally well-developed you think your children are, and possibly how much your parents projected their worries on to you.

Vigilance is important – but then so is freedom. As a dad of four daughters, I know what it's like to feel you have to protect them. But I also know I'm not going to be here forever, so it's important to equip them to face the world. They've been extremely fortunate to have, as a role model, a mother who encouraged them to have their own opinions and to speak up for what they believe in.

YOUR EXAMPLE IS THE ONE THAT MATTERS

I believe it's important to acknowledge that you can't be the *perfect* parent. If you accept that, you will be easier on yourself and a whole lot easier on your children. If you continually criticise yourself then you're in danger of being overly critical of your children and that's not good. I'm aware that I'm highly self-critical and that if I were to let this get out of control it would not be healthy for the girls.

I don't think many of us realise what power we have over children. Sure we're up against other influences, such as the media, peer group pressure, teachers and other parents (who might be much 'cooler' than us), but the fact remains that you are in the best position of all to influence your children. Never mind what goes on outside the home. Children are more likely to smoke if their parents smoke, more likely to be overweight if their parents are overweight, and more likely to develop an alcohol or drug problem if they're exposed to them at home. It's that simple.

We all have our own views, of course, but my opinion is that you can't get there by manipulating through reward and punishment. That's partly because children are smart and know exactly what you're doing. I'm not sure that we were working to a plan exactly, but, looking back, I think much of what my ex-wife and I have done is about setting an example. The girls have seen their mother and me work hard for what we have, and they've also seen us getting involved in our communities and doing charity work. In many ways, I think that is more positive and speaks much more loudly than rules and rewards.

Of course, not every example you set will influence your children. I've never been one to trash hotel rooms just because they belong to someone else. Even if I'm enjoying a brief stay, I like to unpack and put all my possessions in to the appropriate drawers and wardrobe. It makes me feel good. It makes me happy. I think I'm making the most of my possessions and the glorious surroundings in which I am fortunate to stay. Contrast this with the behaviour of my daughters, who don't even bother to unpack. It's as if a bomb has gone off deep inside their luggage. They emerge for dinner looking absolutely stunning and immaculate, but how they do it from the wreckage of their travel bags, I've no idea.

THINK AND SPEAK POSITIVELY

Children need to be taught to deal with failure positively. Otherwise how on earth will they cope with the world? While we'd like to believe that our children will live carefree lives devoid of concerns and worries, many children become anxious and self-critical at an early age. This can happen because, as I've seen in my charity work, they have problems or illness in the family. Or it can happen for no reason at all.

Some children seem to be born optimists. They have a wonderful feeling of self-assurance and absolute faith that their wishes and desires will come true. Others have very little faith and worry about everything. If you feel your child has low self-esteem, as evidenced by comments such as, 'I'm not good at anything' or, 'I'm a failure', you should make a conscious attempt to address the problem, rather than hoping they'll grow out of it. You can help by working with them to find something they enjoy doing and that makes them feel proud. It doesn't have to be momentous, just any activity that makes them realise they are good at something.

Of course, in this world of 'parenting' there is enormous pressure on children not just to perform but to out-perform. I suggest that you do yourself and your children a favour and keep away from the 'parenting' people. Recognise and love your children for the individuals they are and do your best to play to their strengths.

I don't know whether my parents had a plan but I do know they always made me feel I was being supported and that even if I couldn't do something well I wasn't useless. In other words, just *trying* meant I wasn't a failure. Earlier on in this book I talked about accepting your unique strengths and not focusing on your weaknesses. The same applies to your children. I know that as parents we all have aspirations for our children, but if we've decided to accept ourselves and now realise that it's not positive to compare our achievements with those of others, then we have to do the same with our children.

DON'T HIDE YOUR FEELINGS

I don't believe in exposing children to every outburst, argument or tirade against the world. I believe those need to be controlled as much for your sake as theirs. But there's no point in pretending that arguments don't happen; your children will soon discover that isn't true. So it's important that they are shown how to resolve an argument and move on.

My daughters have seen their dad come through adversity to become a stronger, more positive individual. As they get older, our relationship is steadily changing to one of friendship, and I find the two eldest are now giving me advice. Apparently I'm getting better at taking it, too!

I hope this chapter demonstrates how my philosophy of positive living translates into one of the most demanding and rewarding things you can do in your life. It's not for me to offer pointers on being a parent; we're all undergraduates when it comes to bringing up children, however I've found that some very simple principles have worked for me.

If you're having a difficult parent moment, don't panic:

- ★ **Accept your limitations and remember, there is no such thing as a perfect parent.**
- ★ **If you're not sure what to do, just listen.**
- ★ **Never forget that you are the best example they have.**
- ★ **Be positive about their achievements no matter how small.**
- ★ **The greatest gift you can give a child is your attention.**
- ★ **If you give them continuous love and security, you have taken them 90% of the way.**
- ★ **Above all… let them be children.**

CHAPTER 8

TWENTY-FIVE WAYS TO BE POSITIVELY HAPPY

WELL, IF YOU'VE GOT this far then you're either curious, contemplating some sort of improvement in your life, or you've opened the book at the back. At this point I think it's time to pull out some key points and put everything together. I want to make it clear that the things I've suggested work for me. But none of this is prescriptive. Don't think you have to do everything at once. Your journey to becoming positively happy is a lifetime one and there will be lots of fine-tuning along the way.

I've been honest in this book because I think being honest with yourself is absolutely vital if you are to be more positive. You also have to believe you have the right to happiness. You cannot and will not do so without this belief. As I said at the beginning, my own belief, that which reinforces my practical actions, lies in the cosmos. But you certainly don't need to believe in the cosmos to understand and follow the concepts in this book. You just need to believe you can do it.

1
CREATE OPPORTUNITIES AND LUCK WILL FOLLOW

In order for good things to happen to you, you have to send the right signals to the cosmos, to other people and to yourself. You can't just sit on your bum and wait for positive things to happen; you have to show that you're worthy of them. People who succeed, actively set out to create opportunities. They don't always know exactly what they want but they don't let that stop them. They just keep trying until they find it.

2
FOCUS ON YOURSELF

You have an obligation to yourself to make your life the best, most productive life you possibly can. Self-focus is the key. It's not about navel gazing or being introspective. Nor is it about being selfish. It's recognising your right to think about yourself and your needs. In this way you will attract opportunity.

3
HAVE A VISION, A PASSION, AN OVERWHELMING DESIRE...

Vision is essential when you are seeking to convert positive thought into success. I cannot think of one significant thing that has happened in my life without my first having a vision of what I wanted. Having a vision is not just day-dreaming: it's having a clear mental picture of what you want and saying, 'That's me. That's where I'm going.' If you don't believe you can do it, nobody else will. You are the one with the vision and you have the power to bring it to life. You need to act like the success you want to be in order to make it happen: self-belief plus a vision of success leads to opportunity. With opportunity comes confidence and success, which breeds even greater success. And thus the cycle continues.

4
MAKE SPACE FOR YOUR DREAMS

You have to make space for what you want and show yourself and others that you are serious. If you don't ask, you don't get. In order to ask for something, you have to positively make room for it in your life. In other words, you have to create the space that allows the opportunity. No matter what other responsibilites you have in life, the one to yourself is just as important as any of them.

5
LET GO OF SELF-IMPOSED LIMITATIONS

Many of our limitations are a result of our upbringing and get reinforced by friends and family, so they can be pretty tough to leave behind. But these are only parameters that we've set for ourselves and, in doing so, we've made them realities. Changing our behaviour means undoing those years of conditioning and altering our views about what we can do. It means liberating ourselves from our past and ultimately becoming more comfortable with who we are.

6
MEMORISE THIS

'Hang on, I am a special person. I am allowed to be happy in what I do. I am allowed to consider my own happiness as well as that of the people around me. And I am allowed to do all of this without feeling guilty.'

7
DON'T DEPEND ON OTHERS FOR APPROVAL

Sure, it's great if others happen to give their approval, but don't go around from person to person looking for it like a little kid at Hallowe'en. You simply cannot rely on others to provide your sense of self-worth. They won't always tell you what you want to hear.

They won't always be there. And they're not you. Remember that you have to fulfil your obligations to yourself. Seriously, though, you have one life and if you don't follow the path you desire, whose life are you living?

8
LIVE THE LIFE YOU'RE LIVING NOW – IT'S THE ONE THAT MATTERS

You do yourself no favours if you dissipate your energies worrying about what has gone before. Before you get to the end of this book, I want you to accept that you cannot do anything about the past. Therefore dwelling on what might have been is taking up time that you could be using to move forwards. It will make you unhappy, angry and frustrated. It will hold you back. You cannot change the past. But you can do something about the present. The ability to live in the here and now is one of the secrets of true happiness

9
THINK LIKE A STRONG PERSON

There, I've labelled you – so now you're stuck with it! There are no strong or weak people. People who are stronger just see things in a different way. Sooner or later things do go wrong and the way we survive these episodes depends on how we choose to view them. You are not a victim. Don't spend too much time trying to analyse. Some things are just the way they are.

10
MAKE SOMEBODY ELSE'S LIFE HAPPIER

People who consider others and engage with them are more likely to have happy lives.

Do something for somebody you don't know. Call it spontaneous positivity; it will make a difference to them. It is contagious. The recipient of spontaneous positivity will become a donor. And you will benefit in ways you could never foresee. When we give of ourselves the returns for everybody are immeasurable. Imagine how we could change the world if everybody engaged in spontaneous positivity just once a week.

11
BE THE POSITIVE FORCE IN YOUR COMMUNITY

There's no point complaining about it and expecting others to do it. Everyone knows that our local communities need to function well in order to ensure that people have the services, security and safety they need to live happy lives. Why shouldn't you be the one to take action?

Community spirit shouldn't be something we show in disasters; it should be there all the time. You can sit around waiting for it to surface – or you can be the one with the spirit. Remember that you have as much power as anybody else.

12
BE GRATEFUL FOR WHAT YOU ALREADY HAVE

Your loved ones might already know you love them but, just to make sure, why not tell them. Don't take these important people for granted. Be grateful for what they've given you. Send them a present or a letter – just because. Remind yourself how grateful you are for everything you have. Write it down on a piece of paper and put it next to your bed. Read it every night.

Don't constantly ask, 'Is that all there is?' If you think like that it just might be. Your happiness shouldn't necessarily be dependant on getting bigger/better/more. If you're not able to see the joy in what you already have, then nothing will make you happy.

13
DO TALK TO STRANGERS

The world is no more or less evil than it ever has been. The majority of people are decent and good and are not out to get you. A stranger is often a friend in waiting. Don't be afraid to acknowledge them and make connections with a fellow being. Someone has to start the conversation.

A human being who does not have contact with

others soon disintegrates into despair, becoming selfish and lonely along the way. Don't let your fears or inadequacies keep you from connecting with the world. Engaging with others in a positive way, whether it's your neighbour, your community or someone you've never met, is the difference between merely existing and really living.

14
DON'T COMPARE YOURSELF TO OTHERS

Don't undermine your efforts by comparing yourself with other people. Constantly looking at what others are doing is not the route to self-acceptance. Yet accepting who you are is one of the most liberating things you can do for yourself.

Just because good fortune smiles upon a neighbour or colleague, it doesn't mean bad fortune is looking down on you. The two situations are not parts of the same equation. Your moment will come, but if you're too busy looking at what others have, you might miss it.

15
ACCEPT THERE IS NO PERFECT LIFE

Strive to make the most of what you have, physically, mentally and emotionally. Don't waste energy on comparing your own life with that of others.

Everything in life has its trade-offs. A life that looks

enviable and fabulous on the outside has its own problems. Others are not having a better time than you are; they probably just don't show their insecurities. And some of them probably think you're having a better time than they are. Life is funny like that.

16
DON'T EXPECT TOO MUCH OF MONEY

Money is money. It is not compensation for anything else. No amount of it can bring you emotional happiness. Money is nice to have but it should not be the sole reason you strive to achieve.

17
BE PROUD OF WHAT YOU'VE DONE SO FAR

I know this is the UK and we're not supposed to shout it from the rooftops, but you are entitled to be proud of what you've achieved. Remember that you're comparing you with you. That's not boasting.

18
PLAY TO YOUR STRENGTHS

Concentrate on the skills and attributes that come most easily to you *and* that you enjoy using. If something is right for you – whether it's a job or a relationship – you won't have to struggle to make it work. If you try to squeeze yourself into something that isn't meant for you, it just won't work.

Getting it right means working out what really matters to you first of all. Be true to yourself and do the very best you can, no matter what you do. Not only will others appreciate you more, *you* will appreciate you more.

19
REMEMBER, YOU'RE HERE FOR A GOOD TIME, NOT A LONG TIME

Life is short and for me that is reason enough not to allow negativity to dominate it. Negative moments are a part of life but dwelling on them need not be. You may also need to think about distancing yourself from negative people. There are people who simply cannot and will not think positively, no matter what happens in their life. These people are not good for you. They'll not only suffocate your ideas, they'll also suffocate you. Remove yourself from them and see how things improve.

20
USE CRITICISM CONSTRUCTIVELY, NOT DESTRUCTIVELY

Making relationships better, be they at work or at home, requires that you learn to give criticism in a constructive manner. Constructive criticism should leave the recipient feeling thoughtful and motivated, not devastated. Remember character assasination says more about your character than the other person.

You become what you practise, and if you practise being spiteful, even to people who don't know that you are doing it, you will become a more negative person yourself.

21
ACCEPT THAT YOU CAN'T BE LIKED BY EVERYONE

Sometimes it's chemistry, sometimes it's the other person's insecurity and their fear of being threatened in some way. Sometimes it's just that they're judgmental, unhappy individuals and they want to take it out on you. Don't fight their negativity with your own.

22
MAKE FRIENDS WITH YOUR LOWS

People who cope with negative feelings don't treat them as something alien. They recognise that lows are just as relevant to life as highs, so they relax and don't waste energy fighting them. Eventually the good times will come around again. If the same thing keeps happening to you, maybe it's time to look a little deeper. Instead of getting frustrated and upset, try to discover why you keep ending up on your head from time to time.

23
SEEK OUT NEW POINTS OF VIEW

If you want to learn how to bring about change in your own life, you can develop flexibility by looking at a situation from a different perspective. You will invariably learn something new. And you will condition yourself not to be so stubborn and resistant to new ideas. You'll also be better prepared to cope with the idea of change.

24
DON'T BE AFRAID OF CHANGE

We spend much of our lives seeking security so it's no surprise that many of us find the idea of change quite scary. But change is not always negative. It can also be a chance to discover new dimensions to our character and free ourselves of self-imposed limitations. If we are brave enough to allow even a small amount of uncertainty into our lives, we have more chance of discovering new avenues of satisfaction and happiness. You have to speculate to accumulate.

25
BELIEVE THAT YOU CAN BE POSITIVELY HAPPY!

I want to make it clear that none of this is prescriptive so please don't think you have to take all this on board at once. Start by picking out five things that you want to do/improve/change and get comfortable with them. Then, when you're ready, move on bit by bit. Your journey to becoming positively happy is a lifetime one and there will be lots of fine-tuning along the way.

I hope that by reading this book you can, at the very least, get to the point where you believe you have the power to redirect your life and become a happier person.

Well, that's just about it. You now know a little bit more about me and a whole lot more about positivity. So there remains just one all-important question – what are you going to do now? Close the cover and hurl the book into the nearest waste bin? Use it to prop up that dodgy coffee table? Or, keep it close to you and regularly refer to the little tips sprinkled through its pages? I really hope it's the latter.

I'd like to leave you with a simple observation on life that has consistently worked for me: the challenges we face everyday do not make us who we are, they reveal who we are. Oh, and never forget that you have a fundamental right to love and be loved, to be successful and to be happy.

Noel Edmonds

INDEX